W9-CZU-317

The Masterworks of Literature Series

Sylvia E. Bowman, *Editor*
Indiana University

The Best of Bill Nye's Humor

The Best of Bill Nye's Humor

Selections from the Nineteenth-Century American Humorist

by BILL NYE

Edited for the Modern Reader by
Louis Hasley
UNIVERSITY OF NOTRE DAME

College & University Press · *Publishers*
NEW HAVEN, CONN.

Library of Congress Catalog Card Number: 73-168388

New Material, Introduction and Notes
by LOUIS HASLEY

MANUFACTURED IN THE UNITED STATES OF AMERICA BY
UNITED PRINTING SERVICES, INC.
NEW HAVEN, CONNECTICUT

TO

LUCILE, SUSAN, JANET, DAN, AND MY STUDENTS
IN THE LITERATURE OF AMERICAN HUMOR

LOUIS HASLEY, *Editor*

Contents

Introduction

A nation's heritage is forever in the process of being lost. The onrush of the crowded present, with its multifarious conflicts, national crises, community and domestic concerns, job pressures, and personal commitments, tends to sweep the past into oblivion. A nation that wishes to preserve its heritage must therefore be constantly engaged, as part of its constructive labor, in sifting the past in order to recover values that would otherwise be lost. No man, invention, custom, or work of art that once had widespread influence over a period of years should be allowed to perish from the collective memory.

The role played by indigenous humor in the development of the American character has been so widely recognized in this century that no case, in the round, need be made for it. No study of American life and culture is complete without it; and no study can afford to ignore the work of such scholars as Constance Rourke and Walter Blair, to mention only two of many who have made outstanding contributions toward recognizing the role humor has played and will continue to play.

It is not, however, merely in the narrowly historical realm that American humor has left us its heritage, nor even in the broader academic field of American Studies. While its casualness, its earthiness, and perhaps its irreverent impudence disqualify it from being classed as *belles lettres*, the best of it—and the amount is considerable—has found warm welcome in the pages of American literature anthologies, and to readers who have seldom had much use for *belles lettres* anyhow. To remember names like Augustus Baldwin Longstreet, James Russell Lowell, Mark Twain, Joel Chandler Harris, George Ade, Ring Lardner, and James Thurber is to think in terms of literature—of writings that are enjoyed over scores of years, not for paraphrasable content, but for enjoyment inseparable from the form in which that content is expressed. Among such writers Bill Nye is one.

I

The history of early American humor shows it to have been under the same influence of the mother literature that most traditional American writing of that time manifested. Most of the writings of Edward Taylor, Jonathan Edwards, Benjamin Franklin, Washington Irving, and Edgar Allan Poe were in the broad manner and temper much like the work of their British contemporaries. So, too, before the publication of *Georgia Scenes* by Longstreet in 1835, we find little humorous writing of literary quality that has the American accent or, with the exception of Irving, any notable humorous accent at all. From 1835, however, until shortly after the Civil War, native voices sounded not only Down East with the shrewd twang of the New England Yankee but also in the backwoods and along the inland rivers with the uninhibited, exuberant, "spontenacious" stories and "brags" that related unparalleled feats of hunters, bargers, frontier politicians, gamblers, horse thieves, lovers, practical jokers, lawyers, preachers, and traveling men. Besides the one volume of Longstreet, the works of William Tappan Thompson, Johnson Jones Hooper, Thomas Bangs Thorpe, and George W. Harris are especially significant.

Following the Civil War, a new group of humorous writers with a different orientation appeared. Aptly characterized as Literary Comedians, they include a numerous brood—notably, such writers as Artemus Ward, Mark Twain (whose work is much wider, however, than this category),

Joel Chandler Harris, Josh Billings, Bill Nye, and Finley Peter Dunne. While it is difficult, if not impossible, to discern among them specific traits in common, it may be fair to say that, as contrasted with the first-growth native humorists before them, most of them are on the whole less spontaneous, more self-conscious; less humorous but wittier; more versatile; less the fabricators of fiction than the commentators on personal tastes and experience; and more inclined to display their wares in the guise of dialect, the vernacular, intentionally bad grammar, puns, malapropisms, and misspellings. In a word, they are more inclined to verbal humor as opposed to situation and character humor. The conversational tones and rhythms of platform performance are also more clearly evident, as in the popular stage monologues begun in 1861 by Artemus Ward and followed by Mark Twain, Bill Nye, and other popular humorists who trod the boards to applause that shook the rafters in the remaining decades of the century.

The purpose of this book is to contribute to a needed rehabilitation of Nye's reputation, which has—unjustifiably, I believe—been at low ebb for four or five decades. One searches in vain the periodical indexes for separate analytical articles devoted wholly to Nye. At best, he is bundled in with such colleagues as Artemus Ward, Josh Billings, and Petroleum V. Nasby and given a collective treatment as one of the satellites in a Twainian universe. Yet Nye does not fit well the stereotype; he has been, to some extent, the victim of erroneous criticism by several acknowledged authorities on humor.

To judge from Canadian Stephen Leacock's widely recognized *Humor and Humanity*, for example, Nye is impliedly a notable punster: "Bill Nye, who flourished at a time when puns were still permitted, and even enjoyed in America. . . ." But puns are remarkably few in Nye, a scarcity which is not necessarily a virtue since Homer, Shakespeare, Thoreau, and the most widely read contemporary American humorous fictionist, Peter De Vries, do not scorn the pun. Agnes Repplier, in her *Pursuit of Laughter*, classifies Nye as a "misspelling" humorist, which he was not, even though most of his colleagues were. Moreover, Miss Repplier says also that "he dealt largely in that exaggeration which has been discredited by sophisticated wits, and which Mrs. Meynell assures us we should resent because it appeals to our credulity. But pioneers delighted in its childishness, which made no appeal whatever to anyone's credulity." Clearly, the childishness mentioned by Miss Repplier is intended pejoratively, though reputable criticism that objects to a similar "childishness" of exaggeration as practiced by Mark Twain would, I think, be hard to find.

II

The little town of Shirley, Maine, was the birthplace of Edgar Wilson (Bill) Nye on August 25, 1850. His parents were Franklin and Elizabeth Mitchell Loring Nye. His father, who was a lumberman, could trace the family line back to England and to thirteenth-century Denmark. Benjamin, the first American Nye, came to Massachusetts from England in 1635. Two years after Edgar's birth, the family moved westward to a farm in St. Croix County, Wisconsin, which is described by the later humorist as "a hundred and sixty acres of beautiful ferns and bright young rattlesnakes." The young Nye, growing up there, attended ("between Indian massacres," he wrote) the district school and also something like our present high school. He then studied for a sixteen-week term at an academy and for two long terms at a military school in River Falls.

His formal schooling over, Nye tried successively a variety of occupations—farming, milling, school teaching, dabbling in journalism, and reading for the law. After failing several times to pass the Wisconsin bar, he went west in 1876 to Laramie City (now Laramie), Wyoming, where an influential friend got him a job at twelve dollars a week as editor of the *Sentinel.* At that time Laramie had a population of about 2500, having been settled by Union Pacific

Railway employees in 1867. In Laramie, Nye was able to pass an informal bar examination; and, while he practiced law but briefly, if at all, he was soon an elected justice of the peace, coroner ex-officio, notary public, and, for two years, United States Commissioner.

Meanwhile, through the matchmaking capacity of Mrs. J. H. Hayford, the wife of Nye's employer, Nye had met an attractive visitor from Illinois, Clara Frances Smith, whose parents had formerly lived near Troy, New York. On March 7, 1877, only a few months after meeting, they were married. The Cheyenne *Sun* reported that "Nye forgot all his jokes suitable to the occasion, and will hereafter be known as the obituary editor of the *Sentinel*." Here is public evidence that Nye, less than a year after landing in Laramie, had already achieved some local fame as a humorist.

Nye's marriage to "Fanny" Smith was a happy one to which were born seven children. There were five boys and two girls, one boy dying as a baby and another being stillborn; the youngest boy was born after his father's death.

Edgar Wilson Nye's *nom-de-plume* of Bill Nye was thrust upon him through the contemporary fame of Bret Harte's fictitious Bill Nye in the classic light verse poem, "Plain Language from Truthful James," published in 1870. Nye indicates somewhat vaguely that the label was affixed by newspapers that had printed some of his early but unsigned humorous pieces. Whatever the circumstances of his use of the name, it was a happy, easy, and memorable handle.

During the seven years Nye spent in Laramie, he began to contribute humor to the Denver *Tribune*. These pieces were often widely copied and soon his fame was burgeoning. It was, however, his founding and editing, in 1881, of a daily paper called the *Boomerang*, and then in addition a *Weekly Boomerang*, that brought his writings to a nationwide public. The papers were named after Nye's own mule, Boomerang. After a successful start, the paper was moved to the loft of a livery stable. "You could come up the stairs into the office," wrote Nye, "or you could twist the tail of the iron gray mule and take the elevator."

As Professor Walter Blair points out in a valuable, well-documented article,[1] almost every important daily newspaper in the country had its humorous staff writer, and newspapers reprinted freely the writings of the best humorists published by rival newspapers. A talented humorist such as Nye readily achieved a nationwide public, for he was copied widely—and not only in his own country but also in England. His work was eventually syndicated in England, where it was also given book publication. After Nye's death in 1896, Orlando Smith, head of the Press Association, declared that "Bill Nye was the most widely read and highly paid writer in the United States."[2] Professor Blair, the best of many authorities on nineteenth-century American humor, characterizes Nye as the last great figure of the old school.

In the second year of *Boomerang*, Nye suffered an attack of cerebrospinal meningitis, causing him to give up his connection with the paper. Meantime, however, a nation's laughter had greeted publication and wide reprinting of his letter to the office of the postmaster-general accepting the appointment as postmaster of Laramie, a job which Nye took seriously but held less than fourteen months. Burdened with heavy duties and advised, because of his illness, to seek a lower altitude, he moved briefly to Greeley, Colorado, and then returned to Wisconsin. His letter of resignation as postmaster, characteristically addressed to President Arthur, stands with his acceptance letter as an American humorous classic.

Nye's first two books, *Bill Nye and Boomerang* and *Forty Liars and Other Lies*, were collections of his journalistic humor. These works had appeared before he left Wyoming to return via Colorado to Wisconsin. During the last ten years of his life, 1886-96, he spent a great deal of time on the lecture circuit in various cities of the United

[1] Walter Blair, "The Popularity of Nineteenth-Century American Humorists," *American Literature*, III (May, 1931), 175-94.

[2] *Ibid.*, p. 192.

States. Four of these very popular years were spent in happy partnership with the Hoosier poet, James Whitcomb Riley. In a given platform appearance they alternated, Nye with humor, Riley with homely, sentimental verse. In a letter to a friend, Riley commented on Nye as a lecturer: "Nye is simply superb on the stage—and no newspaper report can half-way reproduce either the curious charm of his drollery—his improvisations—inspirations and so forth. At times his auditors are hysterical with delight. We repeat tonight by special request of everybody. Newspapers all sent reporters, quite an audience in themselves, as they sat in betabled phalanx in the orchestra-pen, and laughed and whooped and yelled and cried, wholly oblivious of their duty half the time."[3]

As a surprise feature at one of the Riley-Nye performances in Boston, Nye and Riley were introduced to the audience by Mark Twain, who had traveled there especially to hear them. Twain, who gave them an elaborately clever introduction, used the image of inseparable Siamese Twins. As to Nye in particular, he said that "as he is a little lame, I am going to ask you to allow him to speak in a low voice."

During the busy and demanding seasons on the platform, a new collection of Nye's writings appeared almost every year. Sometimes, instead of a new collection, it was a reprint under a new title. In 1887, Nye went to work for the New York *World*, which required him to live in New York City. He moved his now growing family to Staten Island. Two years later he paid his first of two visits to Europe, sent there by the *World* to report the Paris Exposition.

Returning to the United States, Nye resumed the lecture circuit, drawing heavily on his sagging energies and experiencing frequent and excruciating headaches that sometimes required morphine to ease the pain. In the last five years of his life, his home was a few miles south of Asheville, North

[3] *Bill Nye: His Own Life Story*, continuity by Frank Wilson Nye (New York, 1926), p. 146. I am much indebted to this book.—Ed.

Carolina, first at the tiny town of Skyland, and finally at an elaborate gingerbread country mansion which he built and called "Buck Shoals." His letters testify that as always, but never so richly as on his country estate, he enjoyed the companionship of his family, especially that of his two young boys, Max and the one whose name was Frank but who was nicknamed Jim because of the family enthusiasm for their close friend, James Whitcomb Riley.

For three years preceding his death from a stroke on Washington's Birthday, 1896, Bill Nye had been under the care of the family physician who later reported that Nye had been anticipating the end "for some time." He is buried in the Calvary Episcopal Churchyard at Fletcher, North Carolina.

III

It would be hard to find a man better qualified than Edgar Wilson Nye to reflect the various kinds of life in the sections of this country during the latter half of the nineteenth century. Born "Down East" in New England, he grew up in the Midwest, found his life's career in journalism while living in the West, lived for several years in the nation's largest city, traveled and lectured all over the country, and spent the final five years of his life in the South. A gregarious man of great personal magnetism, he made friends everywhere, enjoyed people, and was lovingly devoted to his wife and children. His friendships and other concerns, recorded his son Frank Wilson Nye, caused him to write an average of fifty letters a week, none of them dictated.

In a letter to his lecture agent, Major J. B. Pond, who was also Twain's agent, Nye declared his admiration for his great contemporary. "Tell Mark Twain that if he had not possessed the fatal gift of humor he might now be President of the United States, and if I could have had my way he should have been anyway." However, if we can believe Walt McDougall, an artist who was an illustrator-partner to weekly articles by Nye syndicated by the American Press Association, there was a coolness between Nye and Twain, at least on the part of Twain. "Mark Twain," McDougall wrote in the September, 1925, *American Mercury*, "was decidedly jealous of Nye, who despite the uncouth presentment by which I made his figure known, was both attractive and dignified, his gravity in delightful contrast to the absurd quaintness of his diction. Mark always tried to avoid meeting Nye, and when compelled to by circumstances he was none too genial."

Tributes by Nye's son Frank Wilson Nye and by Nye's brother, Frank Mellen Nye, are apt to sound overly laudatory, but they are supported by Nye's many friends. "He was youthful always, a boy in spirit and disposition to the last. . . . Whether at the unpretentious party, the spelling school, the lyceum, or in the threshing crew, he was the central figure. He drew to him the old and the young. There was beauty in his homeliness, gentility in his awkwardness, philosophy in his jests, good nature in his anger, buoyancy and good cheer in his adversity, wisdom in his youth and youthfulness in his age."[4] Though the quotation just given comes from Bill Nye's brother, I must conclude that it speaks truth. The same source went on to say: "He caricatured the follies and the weaknesses of man. This he did in a general, and never in a personal way. There was no element of bitterness in his nature. He cherished no enmities. He had no time to hate."[5]

After reading this statement, we wonder whether or not Frank had read the several Bill Nye satires mocking Jay Gould. And what would Frank say about Bill Nye's bitterly acidulous condemnations of the Indian character? Oblique and "slantendicular" references in various Nye essays imply that he had both first- and second-hand experiences with the Indian. At any rate, he is often ready to drop his spirit of cheerful fun and switch to satire, or even recrimination,

[4] *Ibid.*, p. 407, quoting the Honorable Frank Mellen Nye.

[5] *Ibid.*

when he approaches the subject. His essay "The Annual Wail" begins:

> As usual, the regular fall wail of the eastern press on the Indian question, charging that the Indians never committed any depredations unless grossly abused, has arrived. We are unpacking it this morning and marking the price on it. . . . It will be closed out very cheap. . . . We are selling Boston lots with large brass-mounted words, at two and three cents a pound. . . .
>
> Every man who knows enough to feed himself out of a maple trough, knows, or ought to know, that the Indian is treacherous, dishonest, diabolical and devilish in the extreme, and that he is only waiting the opportunity to spread out a little juvenile hell over the fair face of nature if you give him one-sixteenth of a chance. He will wear pants and comb his hair, and pray and be a class leader at the agency for fifty-nine years, if he knows that in the summer of the sixtieth year he can murder a few Colorado settlers and beat out the brains of the industrious farmers.[6]

In an earlier Nye essay, "Gingerbread Poems and Cold Pickled Facts," published in his first book (*Bill Nye and Boomerang*, 1881), some strong animadversions on the Indian had already appeared. "And if any ignorant upstart of the frontier, who feels a little sore over the loss of his family [killed by the Indians], undertakes to defraud these wild, free sons of the forest of any or all of their rights, let the lop-eared, slab-sided, knock-kneed, cross-eyed, spavined, lantern-jawed, sway-backed, mangy, flannel-mouth poet of the educated and refined East write poetry about him till he is glad to apologize."

Nye not only vented strong feelings against Jay Gould and the Indians but also, in a number of essays, attacked the Mormon Church. In one of these, he spoke of "the great national abscess known as the Church of Jesus Christ of Latter Day Saints." One doesn't have to read far in Bill Nye to find him capable of invective and satire, as well as of irony that is far from bland. Nevertheless, we cannot

[6] In *Baled Hay*, 1884.

accept the judgment of so prominent an educator as John Dewey, who declared that Nye was a great satirist.[7]

IV

Nye's virtues lay elsewhere, principally in the realm of the journalistic personal essay. The pronoun *I* occurs with great frequency in his writings; for, like other literary comedians, he knew that his capital represented an engaging personal character and image. And discounting the playful embroidery and fascinating exaggerations, we do not encounter in Nye's writings the unreliable persona that appears so often in twentieth-century writers, humorous or otherwise. Nye's cleverness is open and honest; he is his own selfless, favorite victim; and his subjects are perennially those of the personal essayist. The best of what he wrote would often make excellent casuals for today's *New Yorker* magazine, containing as they do capsule insights into human life in general and American life in particular. Wasn't it an eminent impressionist French critic and novelist who said to a group he was addressing: "This afternoon I am going to talk to you *about myself* on the subject of Shakespeare." Such a ploy could well be applied to Bill Nye, allowing him to say: "In this book I am going to talk to you about myself on the subjects of Indians, travel, mining, politics, railroads, schools, Mormons, astronomy, picnics, mules, escapades I have known about or indulged in, law, newspapering, business, love, dueling, weather, cats, humor, servants, great men, history, farming, polygamy, and just about anything in this country of ours that could be caught in my sieve-like mind or be subjected to my elastic imagination."

At his best—any writer is entitled to be judged by his best—his language is the product of an unfettered, often highly fanciful proliferative imagination that is delicious in its freshness:

[7] In *Bill Nye: His Own Life Story, supra*, xiii.

> Cigarette smoking produces a flabby and endogenous condition of the optic nerve, and constant listening at a telephone, always with the same ear, decreases the power of the other ear till it finally just stands around drawing its salary, but actually refusing to hear anything. Carrying an eight-pound cane makes a man lopsided, and the muscular and nervous strain that is necessary to retain a single eyeglass in place and keep it out of the soup, year after year, draws the mental stimulus that should go to the thinker itself, until at last the mind wanders away and forgets to come back, or becomes atrophied, and the great strain incident to the work of pounding sand or coming in when it rains is more than it is equal to.[8]

Or we have his imaginative *reductio ad absurdum* when he speaks of the difficulty of curing spinal meningitis, from which he himself suffered, but which he bore with patient and cheerful courage: "If [the spinal cord] could be taken out, and hung over a clothes line and cleansed with benzine, and then treated with insect powder, or rolled in corn meal, or preserved in alcohol, and then put back, it would be all right, but you can't. You pull a man's spine out of his system and he is bound to miss it, no matter how careful you have been about it."[9]

In the line of charm-filled nonsense, a discussion of artificial noses yields these comments: "The wax nose is attractive, but in a warm room it is apt to get excited and wander down into the moustache. . . . A gold nose that opens on one side and is engraved, with hunter case and key wind, is attractive, especially on a bright day."[10]

When Nye considers the "great colic promoter," the midsummer cucumber, his imagination follows as the cucumber is eaten by a girl (who, incidentally, has 495 needles in her stomach): "We can imagine the cheerful smile of the cucumber as it enters the stomach, and bowing cheerfully to the follicles standing around, hangs its hat upon the walls

[8] "The Dubious Future," in *A Guest at the Ludlow*, 1897.

[9] "Spinal Meningitis," in *Bill Nye's Remarks*, 1887.

[10] "The Dubious Future," in *A Guest at the Ludlow*, 1897.

of the stomach, stands its umbrella in a corner and proceeds to get in its work."[11]

Of course, in common with most American humorists of his century, Nye indulged freely in exaggeration: "Two of us finally concluded to play billiards, but we were only amateurs and the owner intimated that he would want the table for Fourth of July, so we broke off in the middle of the first game and I paid for it."[12] The reader is perhaps reminded here of the three baseball players indulging in billiards with Ring Lardner's famed, fictional Alibi Ike: "We started out to play fifty points, but we had to make it a thousand so as I and Jack and Carey could try the table."

In the broad technique of mixed figures, or "universe changing," Nye can write of coming home red of eye late at night "with the cork out of my telescope." Or he asserts self-righteously that "I would rather have my right hand cleave to the roof of my mouth than to utter a sentiment that I would regret." He tells of an irate reader who threatens a fearless editor with "a watch pocket under the eye."

Readers frequently enjoy in Nye a device sometimes called "rhapsody." It is marked by Nye's being transparently carried away into eloquence, the tone just suggesting his awareness of comic overtones, as, for example, when the fox hunt in which he was participating went through a "hothouse": "To stand knee-deep in glass and gladiolas, to smell the mashed and mussed up mignonette and the last fragrant sigh of the scrunched heliotrope beneath the hoof of your horse, while far away the deep-mouthed baying of the hoarse hounds, hotly hugging the reeking trail of the anise-seed bag calls on the gorgeously caparisoned hills to give back their merry music or fork it over to other answering hills, is joy to the huntsman's heart."[13]

[11] "A Fatal Thirst," in *Forty Liars, and Other Lies*, 1882.

[12] "Fraternal Sparring," in *Baled Hay*, 1884.

[13] "How to Hunt the Fox," in *Nye and Riley's Railway Guide*, 1888.

Like other literary comedians, Nye often employed the incongruous catalogue, but with him it was likely to stray far into the realm of nonsense, as in "The Modern Parlor Stove":

> After this start your fire, throw open the lemon-squeezer and right oblique hydraulic, see that the tape-worm pinion and Aurora Borealis are well oiled, bring the rotary pitman forward until it corresponds to the maintop mizzen, let go the smoke stack, horizontal duodenum, thorough brace and breech-pin, and as the stove begins to get under way you can slide forward the camera; see that the ramrod is in its place, unscrew the cerebellum, allow the water gauge to run up to about 75° in the shade, keep your eye on the usufruct, and the stove cannot fail to give satisfaction.[14]

Some of Nye's best figures are indebted to the world of religion. One wild comparison tells of persons who do not know "the difference between a 'lower case' *q* and the old Calvinistic doctrine of unanimous damnation." Of his mule, Boomerang, he wrote: "About all the relaxation he has is to induce some trusting stranger to caress his favorite chilblain, and then he kicks the confiding stranger so high that he can count the lamp-posts on the streets of the New Jerusalem."

Among the faults of Nye's highly individualistic and only occasionally distinguished prose are several annoyingly coy mannerisms of style, such as "proclaiming at so much a proclaim," "judging at so much per judge," or overuse (it doesn't take much) of humorously intended expressions such as "pounding sand" and "regardless of expense." Unlike so many of his contemporaries, he rarely stoops to the sin of misspelling with humorous intent. Neither does he use dialect or slang, though at long intervals a bit of vernacular grammar appears ("the proprietor don't ask how much baggage you have"); and also at long intervals a lapse in syntax may occur because of Nye's modest nineteenth-century American education.

[14] In *Bill Nye and Boomerang*, 1881.

V

Like most journalistic humorists (and nearly all literary humorists are first of all journalists), Bill Nye wrote too much and too rapidly. He revised little, fearing loss of spontaneity; and he seemingly had little thought of achieving permanence. Probably at least two-thirds of what he wrote does not merit reprinting today. Yet he is, in a substantial number of pieces, one of the funniest of America's shrewd literary humorists, one who can make many a reader laugh out loud because a live human foible is caught deftly in an ingenuous phrase or because the maverick but true insight is arrived at deviously by surprise or understatement. Nye's prevailing bias is rural and western, and while some critics argue whether or not the West has given us a literature, surely it has given us a mythology of fascination and importance, and to it Nye is a significant contributor.

In a letter to fellow humorist Eli Perkins, Nye declared his purpose to be, "in my poor, weak way, to make folly appear foolish, and to make men better by speaking disrespectfully of their errors." Insofar as his work has significant substance, it is because he caught, on the one hand, a rich segment of frontier local color along the continental divide during the last quarter of the nineteenth century; on the other, because he adopted the new American spirit of challenging and analyzing traditional and conventional ideas.

Apart from the broad body of humorously personalized prose on which Nye's reputation must rest, his work makes no splash. He did write two plays which were produced, *The Cadi* and *The Stag Party*, the first of which ran 125 nights in 1891 at the Union Square Theatre in New York, the second closed after two weeks (1895). What his unpublished novel *Thelma* might have been had it not sunk to the bottom of the Atlantic when Nye was shipwrecked in 1895 off the Bahamas there is no way of knowing. Another genre, however, that he turned to sporadically was light verse; and the several samples scattered throughout his work (I have included only one in this book) reveal a talent for this art that might have achieved success had he chosen to pursue it.

The reader will observe that the individual selections in this book are arranged primarily by topics under eight general headings, and only secondarily, under each of the headings, by book publication chronology (even here I have made several departures from chronology because of grouping pieces on the same general subject). This arrangement is intended to serve the double purpose of allowing the reader's topical interests to be easily satisfied and also making the date of book publication easily accessible by recourse to volume titles and dates given after each selection in the book proper. Chronology in Nye's writings will be seen to be of less than major importance. His later essays are usually longer, having been produced for weekly syndication, as compared to the earlier and ordinarily shorter items produced for daily publication. A sensitive reader may also observe in the later selections a surer, more self-confident vehicle resulting from increased experience and maturity but having lost some spontaneity.

Most of the headings I have chosen should at least recommend themselves for simplicity. That they are not air-tight, logical compartments is obvious. That some of the selections could have been entered under other headings is evident. And it is equally clear that nearly all of them could have been embraced under one heading, "The Human Condition." As the classification process turned out, that eighth and final heading had to be comprehensive so as to accommodate by far the greatest number of items, simply because they couldn't fit under any of the other headings. As for the other headings, perhaps that for the third group, which is also the title of a Charles Lamb essay, "Imperfect Sympathies," sins by speaking more softly than the tenor of Nye's Indian and Mormon excoriations warrants; but we shall let the reader decide. As to the only other heading that might be called vague, "The Muses and Their Kin," a glance at the titles coming under it immediately suggests its intention.

In making a selection from the entire body of Bill Nye's published books, I have had to let my taste in choosing speak for itself. "One man's humor is another man's poison," says Frank Sullivan. For more than fifteen years I have taught a course in the literature of American humor to upper-class college students, and Bill Nye was one of the humorists who always insisted on a place in the course by reason of the pure pleasure to be found in reading him. May I be pardoned for the modest hope that this book will help to preserve, for some scores of years longer, a substantial body of comments on the human condition that seemed otherwise to be slipping away to an undeserved oblivion.

Louis Hasley

University of Natre Dame
March, 1971

CHAPTER *1*

The Great Outdoors

Billious Nye and Boomerang in the Gold Mines

Whenever the cares of life weigh too heavily upon me, and the *ennui* which comes to those who have more wealth than they know what to do with settles down upon me, and I get weary of civilization, I like to load up my narrow-gauge mule Boomerang and take a trip into the mountains. I call my mule Boomerang because I never know where he is going to strike. He is a perpetual surprise to me in this respect. A protracted acquaintance with him, however, has taught me to stand in front of him when I address him, for the recoil of Boomerang is very disastrous. Boomerang is very much below the medium height, with a sad, faraway look in his eye. He has an expression of woe and disappointment and gloom, because life has been to him a series of blasted hopes and shattered ambitions.

In his youth he yearned to be the trick-mule of a circus, and though he fitted himself for that profession, he finds himself in the decline of life with his bright anticipations nothing but a vast and robust ruin. About all the relaxation he has is to induce some trusting stranger to caress his favorite chilblain, and then he kicks the confiding stranger so high that he can count the lamp-posts on the streets of the New Jerusalem. When Boomerang and I visit a mining camp the supplies of giant powder and other combustibles are removed to some old shaft and placed under a strong guard. In one or two instances where this precaution was not taken the site of the camp is now a desolate, barren waste, occupied by the prairie-dog and the jack-rabbit. When Boomerang finds a nitro-glycerine can in the heart of a flourishing camp, and has room to throw himself, he can arrange a larger engagement for the coroner than any mule I ever saw.

There is a new camp in the valley of the Big Laramie River near the dividing line between Wyoming and Colorado. A few weeks ago the murmur of the rapid river down the canon and the cheerful solo of the cayote alone were heard. Now several hundred anxious excited miners are prospecting for gold, and the tent-town grows apace. Up and down the sides of the river and over the side of the mountain every little way a notice greets the eye announcing that "the undersigned claim 1,500 feet in length by 300 feet in width upon" the lode known as the Pauper's Dream, or the Blue Tail Fly, or the Blind Tom, or the Captain Kidd, or the Pigeon-Toed Pete, with all the dips, spurs, angles, gold and silver bearing rock or earth therein contained.

I have a claim further on in the North Park of Colorado. I have always felt a little delicate about working it, because heretofore several gentlemen from the Ute reservation on White River have claimed it. They are the same parties who got into a little difficulty with Agent Meeker and killed him. Of course these parties are not *bona fide* citizens of the United States, and therefore cannot hold my claim under the mining law; but I have not as yet raised the point with them. Whenever they would go over into the park for rest and recreation, I would respect their feelings and withdraw. I didn't know but they might have some private business which they did not wish me to overhear, so I came away.

Once I came away in the night. It is cooler travelling in the night, and does not attract so much attention. Last summer Antelope and his band came over into the park and told the miners that he would give them "one sleep" to get out of there. I told him that I didn't care much for sleep anyhow, and I would struggle along somehow till I got home. I told him that my constitution would stand it first-rate without rest, and I felt as though my business in town might be suffering in my absence. So I went home. The mine is there yet, but I would sell it very reasonably—very reasonably indeed. I do not apprehend any trouble from the Indians, but I have lost my interest in mines to some extent. The Indians are not all treacherous and bloodthirsty as some would suppose. Only the live ones are that way. Wooden Indians are also to be relied upon.

In digging an irrigating ditch on the Laramie Plains last summer, the skeleton of an Indian chief was plowed up. I went to look at him. He had, no doubt, been dead many years; but in the dry alkaline divide, at an elevation of nearly 8,000 feet above sea level, his skull had been preserved pretty well. I took it in my hand and looked it over and shook the sand out of it, and convinced myself that life was extinct. An Indian is not always dead when he has that appearance. I always feel a little timid till I see his scapula, and ribs, and shin bones mixed up so that Gabriel would rather arrange a 15 puzzle than to fix up an Indian out of the wreck. Then I have the most childlike faith and confidence in him. When some avenging fate overtakes a Ute and knocks him into pi, and thus makes a Piute out of him, and flattens him out like a postage stamp, and pulverizes him, and runs him over the amalgator, and assays him so that he lies in the retort like a seidlitz powder, then I feel that I can trust him. I do not care then how much the cold world may scoff at him. Prior to that I am very reserved and very reticent.

That is why I presented my mine to the Ute nation as a slight token of my respect and esteem. Then I went away. I did not hurry much, but I had every inducement and encouragement to reach home at the earliest possible moment, and the result was very gratifying. Very much so, indeed. I left my gun and ammunition, but it did not matter. It wasn't a very good gun anyhow. I do not need it. Anyone going into the park this summer can have it. It is standing behind the door of the cabin between the piano and the whatnot.

(*Bill Nye and Boomerang*, 1881)

My Mine

I have decided to sacrifice another valuable piece of mining property this spring. It would not be sold if I had the necessary capital to develop it. It is a good mine, for I located it myself. I remember well the day I climbed up on the ridge-pole of the universe and nailed my location notice to the eaves of the sky.

It was in August that I discovered the Vanderbilt claim in a snowstorm. It cropped out apparently a little southeast of a point where the arc of the orbit of Venus bisects the milky way, and ran due east eighty chains, three links and a swivel, thence south fifteen paces and a half to a blue spot in the sky, thence proceeding west eighty chains, three links of sausage and a half to a fixed star, thence north across the lead to place of beginning.

The Vanderbilt set out to be a carbonate deposit but changed its mind. I sent a piece of the cropping to a man over in Salt Lake who is a good assayer and quite a scientist if he would brace up and avoid humor. His assay read as follows to-wit:

Salt Lake City, U. T., August 25, 1887

Mr. Bill Nye:—Your specimen of ore No. 35832, current series, has been submitted to assay and shows the following result:

Metal	Ounces	Value per ton
Gold	—	—

Silver	—	—
Railroad iron	1	—
Pyrites of poverty	9	—
Parasites of disappointment	90	—

McVicker, Assayer

NOTE:— I also find that the formation is igneous, prehistoric and erroneous. If I were you I would sink a prospect shaft below the vertical slide where the old red brimstone and preadamite slag cross-cut the malachite and intersect the schist. I think that would be schist about as good as anything you could do. Then send me specimens with $2 for assay and we shall see what we shall see.

Well, I didn't know he was "an humorist," you see, so I went to work on the Vanderbilt to try and do what Mac. said. I sank a shaft and everything else I could get hold of on that claim. It was so high that we had to carry water up there to drink when we began and before fall we had struck a vein of the richest water you ever saw. We had more water in that mine than the regular army could use.

When we got down sixty feet I sent some pieces of the pay streak to the assayer again. This time he wrote me quite a letter, and at the same time inclosed the certificate of assay.

Salt Lake City, U. T., October 3, 1877

Mr. Bill Nye:—Your specimen of ore No. 36132, current series, has been submitted to assay and shows the following result:

Metal	Ounces	Value per ton
Gold	—	—
Silver	—	—
Stove polish	trace	.01
Old gray whitstone	trace	.01
Bromide of axle grease	stain	—
Copperas	trace	5¢ worth
Blue vitrol	trace	5¢ worth

McVicker, Assayer

In the letter he said there was, no doubt, something in the claim if I could get the true contact with calcimine walls denoting a true fissure. He thought I ought to run a drift. I told him I had already run adrift.

Then he said to stope out my stove polish ore and sell it for enough to go on with the development. I tried that but capital seemed coy. Others had been there before me and capital bade me soak my head and said other things which grated harshly on my sensitive nature.

The Vanderbilt mine, with all its dips, spurs, angles, variations, veins, sinuosities, rights, titles, franchises, prerogatives and assessments is now for sale. I sell it in order to raise the necessary funds for the development of the Governor of North Carolina. I had so much trouble with water in the Vanderbilt that I named the new claim the Governor of North Carolina because he was always dry.

(*Bill Nye's Remarks*, 1887)

A Christmas Ride in July

I've just returned from a long ride to the Soda Lakes.

The ride reminded me of a tour I took in July from Laramie over to Cheyenne, two years ago. We had experienced the pleasure of riding over the mountain on the Union Pacific train, and had held our breath while crossing Dale Creek bridge, and viewed with wonder the broken billows of granite, lying here and there at the tip-top of the mighty divide. But some one had said that it was nothing compared with the mirth-provoking trip by carriage across the mountains over a fine wagon road to Cheyenne.

In the morning I nearly melted riding up the sandy canyon, and took off my coat and gliding pleasantly along alternately sang one or two low throbs of melody and alternately swore about the extreme heat.

When we got nearly to the top I thought it didn't look well for a man to whom the American people look for so much in the future to be riding along the public highway without his coat, so I put it on. At the top of the mountain I put on a linen duster and gloves. Shortly after that I put on my overshoes and a sealskin cap. Later, I put on my buffalo overcoat and got out and ran behind the carriage to keep warm.

When I got to Cheyenne, the Doctor looked me over and said that he could save my feet because they had so much vitality, and were in such a good state of preservation; but my ears—my pride and glory—the ears that I had defended through the newspapers for years, and had stood up for when all about was dark—they had to go.

That is, part of them had to go, and there was enough left to hear with; but the ornamental scallops and the box plaiting, and frills, the wainscoating, and royal Corinthian entablatures had to go.

(*Bill Nye and Boomerang*, 1881)

Sliding Down a Mountain in a Gold Pan

Dear reader, did you ever slide down a mountain in a gold pan? Did you ever experience the exhilaration of scooting down the range while the panorama of the great west flew past you like a dream?

Early in the spring a North Park miner, who had been prospecting for gold on the headwaters of the Platte, got up on the continental divide, about 12,000 feet above high water mark, to view the beauties of nature, and as he had heard of the wild, glad intoxication of sliding down hill in a gold pan, he concluded to experience the delightful thrill.

There was really too much thrill to the superficial foot, as he found to his sorrow.

He had, of course, climbed far above snow line, and had a chance to start on an incipient glacier. This gave him a velocity which filled him full of eager surprise.

The speed, as it became more accelerated, took his breath away. There was a good deal of pure mountain air all about him, but he hadn't time to select any. He seemed in a hurry to get there.

On and still on he flew like a wild-eyed meteor, and still he clung convulsively to the gold pan in which he sat.

Anon he got below the snow line and began to scoot over the boulders on the mountain side. This heated the pan to a white heat, and the occupant felt as though someone had knocked him over on a red-hot stove.

* * *

Days passed, and weeks were swallowed up in the filmy night of the irredeemable previously. Weeks grew into months, and still the miner came not to his cabin.

He had been almost forgotten by his companions, when, on the green banks of a mountain stream, the boys, one day, a short time ago, stumbled over a gold pan.

It only contained the copper rivets of a pair of canvas overalls, and a few charred fragments of a fried prospector.

That was all. Silently, and with bowed, uncovered heads, in the midst of the solemn mountain hush, by the banks of the bubbling stream, where the melancholy coyote howls his sad refrain, and where the greasewood and the sagebrush are weeping o'er his final resting place, they planted his remains, and on the candle-box cover, o'er his lonely grave, they wrote with red chalk:

> Over the river on the golden street,
> Slim-nosed William we all shall meet,
> Over the river, on the other side,
> Somewhat disfigured and muchly fried,
> Slim-nosed William has crossed the tide.

(*Forty Liars, and Other Lies*, 1882)

Why We Are Not Gay

It was the policy of this paper, from its inception, whatever that is, to frown upon and discourage fraud wherever the latter has shown its hideous front. In doing so, we have simply done our duty, and our reward has been great, partially in the shape of money, and partially in the shape of conscious rectitude and new subscribers.

We shall continue this course until we are able to take a trip to Europe, or until some large man comes into the office with a masked battery and blows us out through the window into the mellow haze of an eternal summer time.

We have been waiting until the present time for about 100,000 shade trees in this town to grow, and as they seem to be a little reluctant about doing so, and the season being now far advanced, we feel safe in saying that they are dead. They were purchased a year ago of a nursery that purported to be O.K., and up to that time no one had ever breathed a word against it. Now, however, unless those trees are replaced, we shall be compelled to publish the name of that nursery in large, glaring type, to the world. The trees looked a little under the weather when they arrived, but we thought we could bring them out by nursing them. They stood up in the spring breeze like a seed wart, however, and refused to leave. They are still obstinate. The agent concluded to leave, but the trees did not. We feel hurt about it, because people come here from a distance and laugh at our hoe-handle forest. They speak jeeringly of our wilderness of deceased elms, and sneer at our defunct magnolias. We hate to cast a reflection on the house, but we also dislike to be played for Chinamen when we are no such thing.

We prefer to sit in the shade of the luxuriant telegraph pole, and stroll at set of sun amid the umbrageous shadows of the barbed wire fence, through which the sunlight glints and glitters to and fro.

Nothing saddens us like death in any form, and 100,000 dead trees scattered through the city, sticking their limbs up into the atmosphere like a variety actress, bears down upon us with the leaden weight of an ever-present gloom.

(*Baled Hay*, 1884)

On Cyclones

I desire to state that my position as United States Cyclonist for this Judicial District is now vacant. I resigned on the 9th day of September, A. D. 1884.

I have not the necessary personal magnetism to look a cyclone in the eye and make it quail. I am stern and even haughty in my intercourse with men, but when a Manitoba simoon takes me by the brow of my pantaloons and throws me across Township 28, Range 18, West of the 5th Principal Meridian, I lose my mental reserve and become anxious and even taciturn. For thirty years I had yearned to see a grown up cyclone, of the ring-tail-puller variety, mop up the green earth with huge forest trees and make the landscape looked tired. On the 9th day of September, A. D. 1884, my morbid curiosity was gratified.

As the people came out into the forest with lanterns and pulled me out of the crotch of a basswood tree with a "tackle and fall," I remember I told them I didn't yearn for any more atmospheric phenomena. The old desire for a hurricane that would blow a cow through a penitentiary was satiated. I remember when the doctor pried the bones of my leg together, in order to kind of draw my attention away from the limb, he asked me how I liked the fall style of Zephyr in that locality.

I said it was all right, what there was of it. I said this in a tone of bitter irony.

Cyclones are of two kinds, viz: the dark maroon cyclone;

and the iron gray cyclone with pale green mane and tail. It was the latter kind I frolicked with on the above-named date.

My brother and I were riding along in the grand old forest, and I had just been singing a few bars from the opera of "Whoop 'em Up, Lizzie Jane," when I noticed that the wind was beginning to sough through the trees. Soon after that, I noticed that I was soughing through the trees also, and I am really no slouch of a sougher, either, when I get started.

The horse was hanging by the breeching from the bough of a large butternut tree, waiting for some one to come and pick him.

I did not see my brother at first, but after a while he disengaged himself from a rail fence and came where I was hanging, wrong end up, with my personal effects spilling out of my pockets. I told him that, as soon as the wind kind of softened down, I wished he would go and pick the horse. He did so, and at midnight a party of friends carried me into town on a stretcher. It was quite an ovation. To think of a torchlight procession coming way out there into the woods at midnight and carrying me into town on their shoulders in triumph! And yet I was once only a poor boy!

It shows what may be accomplished by anyone if he will persevere and insist on living a different life.

The cyclone is a natural phenomenon, enjoying the most robust health. It may be a pleasure for a man with great will power and an iron constitution to study more carefully into the habits of the cyclone, but as far as I am concerned individually, I could worry along some way if we didn't have a phenomenon in the house from one year's end to another.

As I sit here, with my leg in a silicate of soda corset, and watch the merry throng promenading down the street, or mingling in the giddy torchlight procession, I cannot repress a feeling toward a cyclone that almost amounts to disgust.

(*Bill Nye's Remarks*, 1887)

Skimming the Milky Way

The Comet

The comet is a kind of astronomical parody on the planet. Comets look some like planets, but they are thinner and do not hurt so hard when they hit anybody as a planet does. The comet was so called because it had hair on it, I believe, but late years the bald-headed comet is giving just as good satisfaction everywhere.

The characteristic features of a comet are: A nucleus, a nebulous light or coma, and usually a luminous train or tail worn high. Sometimes several tails are observed on one comet, but this occurs only in flush times.

When I was young I used to think I would like to be a comet in the sky, up above the world so high, with nothing to do but loaf around and play with the little new-laid planets and have a good time, but now I can see where I was wrong. Comets also have their troubles, their perihilions, their hyperbolas and their parabolas. A little over 300 years ago Tycho Brahe discovered that comets were extraneous to our atmosphere, and since then times have improved. I can see that trade is steadier and potatoes run less to tows than they did before.

Soon after that they discovered that comets all had more or less periodicity. Nobody knows how they got it. All the astronomers had been watching them day and night and didn't know when they were exposed, but there was no time to talk and argue over the question. There were two or three hundred comets all down with it at once. It was an exciting time.

Comets sometimes live to a great age. This shows that the night air is not so injurious to the health as many people would have us believe. The great comet of 1780 is supposed to have been the one that was noticed about the time of Caesar's death, 44 B. C., and still, when it appeared in Newton's time, seventeen hundred years after its first grand farewell tour, Ike said that it was very well preserved, indeed, and seemed to have retained all its faculties in good shape.

Astronomers say that the tails of all comets are turned from the sun. I do not know why they do this, whether it is etiquette among them or just a mere habit.

A later writer on astronomy said that the substance of the nebulosity and the tail is of almost inconceivable tenuity. He said this and then death came to his relief. Another writer says of the comet and its tail that "the curvature of the latter and the acceleration of the periodic time in the case of Encke's comet indicate their being affected by a resisting medium which has never been observed to have the slightest influence on the planetary periods."

I do not fully agree with the eminent authority, though he may be right. Much fear has been the result of the comet's appearance ever since the world began, and it is as good a thing to worry about as anything I know of. If we could get close to a comet without frightening it away, we would find that we could walk through it anywhere as we could through the glare of a torchlight procession. We should so live that we will not be ashamed to look a comet in the eye, however. Let us pay up our newspaper subscription and lead such lives that when the comet strikes we will be ready.

Some worry a good deal about the chances for a big comet to plow into the sun some dark, rainy night, and thus bust up the whole universe. I wish that was all I had to worry about. If any respectable man will agree to pay my taxes and funeral expenses, I will agree to do his worrying about the comet's crashing into the bosom of the sun and knocking its daylights out.

The Sun

This luminous body is 92,000,000 miles from the earth, though there have been mornings this winter when it seemed to me that it was farther than that. A railway train going at the rate of 40 miles per hour would be 263 years going there, to say nothing of stopping for fuel or water, or stopping on side tracks to wait for freight trains to pass. Several years ago it was discovered that a slight error had been made in the calculations of the sun's distance from the earth, and, owing to a misplaced logarithm, or something of that kind, a mistake of 3,000,000 miles was made in the result. People cannot be too careful in such matters. Supposing that, on the strength of the information contained in the old time-table, a man should start out with only provisions sufficient to take him 89,000,000 miles and should then find that 3,000,000 miles still stretched out ahead of him. He would then have to buy fresh figs of the train boy in order to sustain life. Think of buying nice fresh figs on a train that had been *en route* 250 years!

Imagine a train boy starting out at ten years of age, and perishing at the age of 60 years with only one-fifth of his journey accomplished. Think of five train boys, one after the other, dying of old age on the way, and the train at last pulling slowly into the depot with not a living thing on board except the worms in the "nice eating apples!"

The sun cannot be examined through an ordinary telescope with impunity. Only one man ever tried that, and he is now wearing a glass eye that cost him $9.

If you examine the sun through an ordinary solar microscope, you discover that it has a curdled or mottled appearance, as though suffering from biliousness. It is also marked here and there by long streaks of light called faculae, which look like foam flecks below a cataract. The spots on the sun vary from minute pores the size of an ordinary school district to spots 100,000 miles in diameter, visible to the nude eye. The center of these spots is as black as a brunette cat, and is called the umbra, so called because it resembles an umbrella. The next circle is less dark and called the penumbra because it so closely resembles the penumbra.

There are many theories regarding these spots, but, to be

perfectly candid with the gentle reader, neither Prof. Proctor* nor myself can tell exactly what they are. If we could get a little closer, we flatter ourselves that we could speak more definitely. My own theory is they are either, first, open air caucuses held by the colored people of the sun; or, second, they may be the dark horses in the campaign; or, third, they may be the spots knocked off the defeated candidate by the opposition.

Frankly, however, I do not believe either of these theories to be tenable. Prof. Proctor sneers at these theories also on the ground that these spots do not appear to revolve so fast as the sun. This, however, I am prepared to explain upon the theory that this might be the result of delays in the returns. However, I am free to confess that speculative science is filled with the intangible.

The sun revolves upon his or her axletree, as the case may be, once in 25 to 28 of our days, so that a man living there would have almost two years to pay a 30-day note. We should so live that when we come to die we may go at once to the sun.

Regarding the sun's temperature, Sir John Herschel* says that it is sufficient to melt a shell of ice covering its entire surface to a depth of 40 feet. I do not know whether he made this experiment personally or hired a man to do it for him.

The sun is like the star spangled banner—as it is "still there." You get up tomorrow morning just before sunrise and look away toward the east, and keep on looking in that direction, and at last you will see a fine sight, if what I have been told is true. If the sunrise is as grand as the sunset, it indeed must be one of nature's most sublime phenomena.

The sun is the great source of light and heat for our

*Richard Anthony Proctor, 1837-88, author of many books on astronomy.—Ed.

*Sir John Frederick William Herschel, 1792-1871, English astronomer and chemist.—Ed.

earth. If the sun were to go somewhere for a few weeks for relaxation and rest, it would be a cold day for us. The moon, too, would be useless, for she is largely dependent on the sun. Animal life would soon cease and real estate would become depressed in price. We owe very much of our enjoyment to the sun, and not many years ago there were a large number of people who worshiped the sun. When a man showed signs of emotional insanity, they took him up on the observatory of the temple and sacrificed him to the sun. They were a very prosperous and happy people. If the conqueror had not come among them with civilization and guns and grand juries they would have been very happy indeed.

The Stars

There is much in the great field of astronomy that is discouraging to the savant who hasn't the time nor means to rummage around through the heavens. At times I am almost hopeless, and feel like saying to the great yearnful, hungry world: "Grope on forever. Do not ask me for another scientific fact. Find it out yourself. Hunt up your own new-laid planets and let me have a rest. Never ask me again to sit up all night and take care of a new-born world while you lie in bed and reck not."

I get no salary for examining the trackless void night after night when I ought to be in bed. I sacrifice my health in order that the public may know at once of the presence of a red-hot comet, fresh from the factory. And yet, what thanks do I get?

Is it surprising that every little while I contemplate withdrawing from scientific research to go and skin an eight-mule team down through the dim vista of relentless years?

Then again, you take a certain style of star which you learn from Professor Simon Newcomb is such a distance that it takes 50,000 years for its light to reach Boston. Now, we will suppose that after looking over the large stock of new and second-hand stars, and after examining the spring catalogue and price list, I decide that one of the smaller size will do me, and I buy it. How do I know that it was there when I bought it? Its cold and silent rays may have ceased 49,000 years before I was born and the intelligence be still on the way. There is too much margin between sale and delivery. Every now and then another astronomer comes to me and says: "Professor, I have discovered another new star and intend to file it. Found it last night about a mile and a half south of the zenith, running loose. Haven't heard of anybody who has lost a star of the fifteenth magnitude, about thirteen hands high, with light mane and tail, have you?" Now, how do I know that he has discovered a brand new star? How can I discover whether he is or is not playing an old, threadbare star on me for a new one?

We are told that there has been no perceptible growth or decay in the star business since man began to roam around through space, in his mind, and make figures on the barn door with red chalk showing the celestial time table.

No serious accidents have occurred in the starry heavens since I began to observe and study their habits. Not a star has waxed, not a star has waned to my knowledge. Not a planet has season-cracked or shown any of the injurious effects of our rigorous climate. Not a star has ripened prematurely or fallen off the trees. The varnish on the very oldest stars I find on close and critical examination to be in splendid condition. They will all no doubt wear as long as we need them and wink on long after we have ceased to wink back.

In 1866 there appeared suddenly in the northern crown a star of about the third magnitude and worth at least $250. It was generally conceded by astronomers that this was a brand new star that had never been used, but upon consulting Argelander's star catalogue and price list it was found that this was not a new star at all, but an old, faded star of the ninth magnitude, with the front breadths turned wrong side out and trimmed with moonlight along the seams. After a few days of phenomenal brightness, it gently ceased to draw a salary as a star of the third magnitude and walked home with an Uncle Tom's Cabin company.

It is such things as this that make the life of the astronomer one of constant and discouraging toil. I have long contemplated, as I say, the advisability of retiring from this field of science and allowing others to light the northern lights, skim the milky way and do other celestial chores. I would do it myself cheerfully if my health would permit, but for years I have realized, and so has my wife, that my duties as an astronomer kept me up too much at night, and my wife is certainly right about it when she says if I insist on scanning the heavens night after night, coming home late with the cork out of my telescope and my eyes red and swollen with these exhausting night vigils, I will be cut down in my prime. So I am liable to abandon the great labor to which I had intended to devote my life, my dazzling genius and my princely income. I hope that other savants will spare me the pain of another refusal, for my mind is fully made up that unless another skimmist is at once secured, the milky way will henceforth remain unskum.

(*Bill Nye's Remarks*, 1887)

Farming in Maine

The State of Maine is a good place in which to experiment with prohibition, but it is not a good place to farm it in very largely.

In the first place, the season is generally a little reluctant. When I was up near Moosehead Lake, a short time ago, people were driving across that body of water on the ice with perfect impunity. That is one thing that interferes with the farming business in Maine. If a young man is sleighriding every night till midnight, he don't feel like hoeing corn the following day. Any man who has ever had his feet frost-bitten while bugging potatoes, will agree with me that it takes away the charm of pastoral pursuits. It is this desire to amalgamate dog days* and Santa Claus that has injured Maine as an agricultural hot-bed.

Another reason that might be assigned for refraining from agricultural pursuits in Maine, is that the agitator of the soil finds when it is too late that soil itself, which is essential to the successful propagation of crops, has not been in use in Maine for years. While all over the State there is a magnificent stone foundation on which a farm might safely rest, the superstructure, or farm proper, has not been secured.

If I had known when I passed through Minnesota and Illinois what a soil famine there was in Maine, I would have brought some with me. The stone crop this year in Maine will be very great. If they do not crack open during the dry weather, there will be a great many. The stone bruise is also looking unusually well for this season of the year, and chilblains were in full bloom when I was there.

In the neighborhood of Pittsfield, the country seems to run largely to cold water and chattel mortgages. Some think that rum has always kept Maine back, but I claim that it has been wet feet. In another article I refer to the matter of rum in Maine more fully.

The agricultural resources of Pittsfield and vicinity are not great, the pincipal exports being spruce gum and Christmas trees. Here also the huckleberry hath her home. But the country seems to run largely to Christmas trees. They were not yet in bloom when I visited the State, so it was too early to gather propcorn balls and Christmas presents.

Here, near Pittsfield, is the birthplace of the only original wormless dried apple pie, with which we generally insult our gastric economy when we lunch along the railroad. These pies, when properly kiln-dried and rivetted, with Ger-

*Hot, uncomfortable days in July and August when the Dog Star rises and sets with the sun.

man silver monogram on top, if fitted out with Yale time lock, make the best fire and burglar-proof wormless pies of commerce. They take the place of civil war, and as a promoter of intestine strife they have no equal.

The farms in Maine are fenced in with stone walls. I do not know why this is done, for I did not see anything on these farms that anyone would naturally yearn to carry away with him.

I saw some sheep in one of these enclosures. Their steel-pointed bills were lying on the wall near them, and they were resting their jaws in the crisp, frosty morning air. In another enclosure a farmer was planting clover seed with a hypodermic syringe, and covering it with a mustard plaster. He said that last year his clover was a complete failure because his mustard plasters were no good. He had tried to save money by using second-hand mustard plasters, and of course the clover seed, missing the warm stimulus, neglected to rally, and the crop was a failure.

Here may be noticed the canvas-back moose and a strong antipathy to good rum. I do not wonder that the people of Maine are hostile to rum—if they judge all rum by Maine rum. The moose is one of the most gamey of the finny tribe. He is caught in the fall of the year with a double-barrel shotgun and a pair of snowshoes. He does not bite unless irritated, but little boys should not go near the female moose while she is on her nest. The masculine moose wears a harelip, and a hat rack on his head to which is attached a placard on which is printed:

PLEASE KEEP OFF THE GRASS.

This shows that the moose is a humorist.

(*Bill Nye's Remarks*, 1887)

Some Facts of Science

A reporter sent out to find the North Pole some years ago has just been heard from. An exploring party recently found portions of his remains in latitude 4-11-44, longitude sou'west by sou' from the pole, and near the remains the following fragment of a diary:

July 1, 1884.—Have just been out searching for a sunstroke and signs of a thaw. Saw nothing but ice floe and snow as far as the eye could reach. Think we will have snow this evening unless the wind changes.

July 2.—Spent the forenoon exploring to the northwest for right of way for a new equatorial and North Pole railroad that I think would be of immense value to commerce. The grade is easy and the expense would be slight. Ate my last dog to-day. Had intended him for the 4th, but got too hungry, and ate him raw with vinegar. I wish I was at home eating pie.

July 3.—We had quite a frost last night, and it looks this morning as though the corn and small fruits must have suffered. It is now two weeks since the last of the crew died and left me alone. Ate the leather ends of my suspenders today for dinner. I did not need the suspenders, anyway, for by tightening up my pants I find they will stay on all right, and I don't look for any ladies to call, so that even if my pants came off by some oversight or other, nobody would be shocked.

July 4.—Saved up some tar roofing and a bottle of mucilage for my Fourth of July dinner, and gorged myself today. The exercises were very poorly attended and the celebration rather a failure. It is clouding up in the west, and I'm afraid we're going to have snow. Seems to me we're having an all-fired late spring here this year.

July 5.—Didn't drink a drop yesterday. It was the quietest Fourth I ever put in. I never felt so little remorse over the way I celebrated as I do today. I didn't do a thing yesterday that I was ashamed of except to eat the remainder of a box of shoe blacking for supper. Today I ate my last boot-heel, stewed. Looks as though we might have a hard winter.

July 6.—Feel a little apprehension about something to eat. My credit is all right here, but there is no competition, and prices are therefore very high. Ice, however, is still firm. This would be a good ice-cream country if there were any demand, but the country is so sparsely settled that a man feels as lonesome here as a greenbacker at a presidential election. Ate a pound of cotton waste soaked in machine oil, today. There is nothing left for tomorrow but ice-water and an old pocket-book for dinner. Looks as though we might have snow.

July 7.—This is a good, cool place to spend the summer if provisions were more plenty. I am wearing a seal-skin undershirt, with three woolen overshirts and two bear-skin vests, today, and when the dew begins to fall I have to put on my buffalo ulster to keep off the night air. I wish I was home. It seems pretty lonesome here since the other boys died. I do not know what I will get for dinner tomorrow, unless the neighbors bring in something. A big bear is coming down the hatchway as I write. I wish I could eat him. It would be the first square meal for two months. It is, however, a little mixed whether I will eat him or he eat me. It will be a cold day for me if he—— ——

* * *

Here the diary breaks off abruptly, and from the chewed-up appearance of the book, we are led to entertain a horrible fear as to his safety.

(*Bill Nye's Chestnuts, Old and New*, 1887)

A Letter of Acceptance

The secretary of the Ashfield Farmers' Club, of Ashfield, Mass., Mr. E. D. Church, informs me by United States mail that upon receipt of my favorable reply I will become an honorary member of that club, along with George William Curtis, Prof. Norton, Prof. Stanley Hall, of Harvard, and other wet-browed toilers in the catnip-infested domain of Agriculture.

I take this method of thanking the Ashfield Farmers' Club, through its secretary, for the honor thus all so unworthily bestowed, and joyfully accept the honorary membership, with the understanding, however, that during the County Fair the solemn duty of delivering the annual address from the judges' stand, in tones that will not only ring along down the corridors of time, but go thundering three times around a half-mile track and be heard above the rhythmic plunk of the hired man who is trying to ascertain, by means of a large mawl and a thumping machine, how hard he can strike, shall fall upon Mr. Curtis or other honorary members of the club. I have a voice that does very well to express endearment, or other subdued emotions, but it is not effective at a County Fair. Spectators see the wonderful play of my features, but they only hear the low refrain of the haughty Clydesdale steed, who has a neighsal voice and wears his tail in a Grecian coil. I received $150 once for addressing a race-track one mile in length on "The Use and Abuse of Ensilage as a Narcotic." I made the gestures, but the sentiments were those of the four-ton Percheron charger, Little Medicine, dam Eloquent.

I spoke under a low shed and rather adverse circumstances. In talking with the committee afterwards, as I wrapped up my gestures and put them back in the shawl strap, I said that I felt almost ashamed to receive such a price for the sentiments of others, but they said that was all right. No one expected to hear an Agricultural Address.

They claimed that it was most generally purely spectacular, and so they regarded my speech as a great success. I used the same gestures afterwards in speaking of "The Great Falling Off Among Bare-Back Riders in the Circuses of the Present Day."

I would also like to be excused from any duties as a judge of curly-faced stock or as an umpire of ornamental needlework. After a person has had a fountain pen kicked endwise through his chest by the animal to which he has awarded the prize, and later on has his features worked up into a giblet pie by the owner of the animal to whom he did not award the prize, he does not ask for public recognition at the hands of his fellow-citizens. It is the same in the matter of ornamental needlework and gaudy quilts, which goad a man to drink and death. While I am proud to belong to a farmers' club and "change works" with a hearty, whole-souled ploughman like George William Curtis, I hope that at all County Fairs or other intellectual hand-to-hand contests between outdoor orators and other domestic animals, I may be excused, and that when judges of inflamed slumber robes and restless tidies, which roll up and fall over the floor to adhere to the backs of innocent people; or stiff, hard Doric pillow-shams which do not in any way enhance the joys of sleep; or beautiful, pale-blue satin pincushions, which it would be wicked to put a pin in and which will therefore ever and forevermore mock the man who really wants a pin, just as a beautiful match-safe stands idly through the long vigils of the night, year after year, only to laugh at the man who staggers towards it and falls up against it and finds it empty; or like the glorious inkstand which is so pretty and so fragile that it stands around with its hands in its pockets acquiring dust and dead flies for centuries, so that when you are in a hurry you stick you pen into a small chamber of horrors—I say when the judges are selected for this department I would rather have my name omitted from the panel, as I have formed or expressed an opinion and have reasonable doubts and conscientious scruples which it would require testimony to remove, and I am not qualified anyway, and I have been already placed in jeopardy once, and that is enough.

Mr. Church writes that the club has taken up, discussed and settled all points of importance bearing upon Agriculture, from the tariff up to the question of whether or not turpentine poured in a cow's ear ameliorates the pangs of hollow horn. He desires suggestions and questions for discussion. That shows the club to be thoroughly alive. It will soon be Spring, and we cannot then discuss these matters. New responsibilities will be added day by day in the way of stock, and we will have to think of names for them. Would it not be well before the time comes for active farm work to think out a long list of names before the little strangers arrive? Nothing serves to lower us in the estimation of our fellow-farmers or the world more than the frequent altercations between owners and their hired help over what name they shall give a weary, wobbly calf who has just entered the great arena of life, full of hopes and aspirations, perhaps, but otherwise absolutely empty. Let us consider this before Spring fairly opens, so that we may be prepared for anything of this kind.

One more point may properly come before the club at its next meeting, and I mention it here because I may be so busy at Washington looking after our other interests that I cannot get to the club meeting. I refer to the evident change in climate here from year to year, and its effect upon seeds purchased of florists and seedsmen generally.

Twenty years ago you could plant a seed according to directions and it would produce a plant which seemed to resemble in a general way the picture on the outside of the package. Now, under the fluctuating influences of irresponsible isotherms, phlegmatic Springs, rare June weather and overdone weather in August, I find it almost impossible to produce a plant or vegetable which in any way resembles its portrait. Is it my fault or the fault of the climate? I wish the club would take hold of this at its next regular meeting. I first noticed the change in the summer of '72, I think. I purchased a small package of early Scotch plaid curled kale with a beautiful picture on the outside. It was as good a picture of Scotch kale as I ever saw. I could imagine how gay and light-hearted it was the day it went up to the studio and had its picture taken for this purpose. A short editorial paragraph under the picture stated that I should plant in quick, rich soil, in rows four inches apart, to a depth of one inch, cover lightly and then roll. I did so. No farmer of my years enjoys rolling better than I do.

In a few weeks the kale came up but turned out to be a canard. I then waited two weeks more and other forms of vegetation made their appearance. None of them were kale. A small delegation of bugs which deal mostly with kale came into the garden one day, looked at the picture on the discarded paper, then examined what had crawled out through the ground and went away. I began to fear then that climatic influences had been at work on the seeds, but I had not fully given up all hope.

At first the plants seemed to waver and hesitate over whether they had better be wild parsnips or Lima beans. Then I concluded that they had decided to be foliage plants or rhubarb. But they did not try to live up to their portraits. Pretty soon I discovered that they had no bugs which seemed to go with them, and then I knew they were weeds. Things that are good to eat always have bugs and worms on them, while tansy and castor-oil go through life unmolested.

I ordered a new style of gladiola eight years ago of a man who had his portrait in the bow of his seed catalogue. If he succeeds no better in resembling his portrait than his gladiolas did in resembling theirs, he must be a human onion whose presence may easily be detected at a great distance.

Last year I planted the seeds of a watermelon which I bought of a New York seedsman who writes war articles winters and sells garden seeds in the Spring. The portrait of this watermelon would tempt most any man to climb a nine-rail fence in the dead of night and forget all else in order to drown his better nature and his nose in its cool bosom. People came for miles to look at the picture of this melon and went away with a pleasant taste in their mouths.

The plants were a little sluggish, though I planted in hills far apart each way in a rich warm loam enriched by everything that could make a sincere watermelon get up and hump itself. The melons were to be very large indeed, with a centre like a rose. According to the picture, these melons generally grew so large and plenty that most everybody had to put side-boards on the garden fence to keep them from falling over into other farms and annoying people who had all the melons they needed. I fought squash bugs, cut worms, Hessian flies, chinch bugs, curculio, mange, pip, drought, dropsy, caterpillars and contumely till the latter part of August, when a friend from India came to visit me. I decided to cut a watermelon in honor of his arrival. When the proper moment had arrived and the dinner had progressed till the point of fruit, the tropical depths of my garden gave up their season's wealth in the shape of a low-browed citron about as large and succulent as a hot ball.

I have had other similar experiences, and I think we ought to do something about it if we can. I have planted the seed of the morning glory and the moon flower, and dreamed at night that my home looked like a florist's advertisement, but when leafy June came a bunch of Norway oats and a hill of corn were trying to climb the strings nailed up for the use of my non-resident vines. I have planted with song and laughter the seeds of the ostensible pansy and carnation, only in tears to reap the bachelor's button and the glistening foliage of the sorghum plant. I have planted in faith and a deep, warm soil, with pleasing hope in my heart and a dark-red picture on the outside of the package, only to harvest the low, vulgar jimson weed and the night-blooming bull thistle.

Does the mean temperature or the average rainfall have anything to do with it? If statistics are working these changes they ought to be stopped. For my own part, however, I am led to believe that our seedsmen put so much money into their catalogues that they do not have anything left to use in the purchase of seeds. Good religion and very fair cookies may be produced without the aid of caraway seed, but you cannot gather nice, fresh train figs of thistles or expect much of a seedsman whose plants make no effort whatever to resemble their pictures.

Hoping that you will examine into this matter, and that the club will always hereafter look carefully in this column for its farm information, I remain, in a sitting posture, yours truly,

Bill Nye

(*Nye and Riley's Railway Guide*, 1888)

CHAPTER **2**

The Animal Kingdom

Apostrophe to an Orphan Mule

Oh! lonely, gentle, unobtrusive mule!
Thou standest idly 'gainst the azure sky,
And sweetly, sadly singeth like a hired man.
  Who taught thee thus to warble
In the noontide heat and wrestle with
Thy deep, corroding grief and joyless woe?
Who taught thy simple heart
Its pent-up, wildly warring waste
Of wanton woe to carol forth upon
    The silent air?
I chide thee not because thy
Song is fraught with grief-embittered
Monotone and joyless minor chords
Of wild, imported melody, for thou
Art restless, woe begirt and
Compassed round about with gloom,
  Thou timid, trusting, orphan mule!
    Few joys indeed are thine,
Thou thrice-bestricken, madly—
Mournful, melancholy mule.
And he alone who strews
Thy pathway with his cold remains
Can give thee recompense
    Of lemoncholy woe.
He who hath sought to steer
Thy limber, yielding tail
Ferninst thy crupper-band
  Hath given thee joy, and he alone.
'Tis true, he may have shot

Athwart the Zodiac, and, looking
O'er the outer walls upon
 The New Jerusalem,
Have uttered vain regrets.
Thou reckest not, O orphan mule,
For it hath given thee joy, and
Bound about thy bursting heart,
And held thy tottering reason
 To his throne.
Sing on, O mule, and warble
In the twilight gray,
Unchidden by the heartless throng,
Sing of thy parents on thy father's side.
Yearn for the days now past and gone:
For he who pens these halting,
Limping lines to thee
Doth bid thee yearn, and yearn, and yearn.

(*Bill Nye and Boomerang*, 1881)

The Rocky Mountain Hog

In speaking of the domestic and useful animals of Laramie, it would not be right to overlook the hog. I do not allude to him as useful at all, but he is very domestic. He is more so than the people seem to demand. I never saw hogs with such a strong domestic tendency as the Laramie hogs have. They have a deep and abiding love for home, all of them, and they don't care whose home it is either.

There is a tremendous pressure of hog to the square inch here. The town is filled with homeless, unhappy and starving hogs. They run between your legs during the day, and stand in your front yard and squeal during the night. Most of them are orphans. When Thanksgiving comes it will bring no joy to them. It will be like any other day. About all the fun they have is to root a gate off the hinges, and then run off with a table cloth in their mouths. We should not be too severe, however, on the hog. What means has he of knowing that there is a city ordinance against his running about town? Kind reader, do you think the innocent little hog would openly violate a law of the land if he knew of its existence? Certainly not. It is pardonable ignorance on the part of the hog, the same as it is with the Indian, which causes him to break over the statutes and ordinances of his country.

Our plan, therefore, is to CIVILIZE THE HOG. Build churches and school houses for him. Educate him and teach him the ways of industry. Put a spade and a plow at his disposal, and teach him to till the soil. The natural impulses of the hog are good, but he has been imposed upon by dishonest white men.

Long before man came with his modern appliances, the hog was here. He owned the land and used it to raise acorns and grub worms on. But the white man has entered on the fair domain, and, regardless of his solemn treaties, has taken this land and asks that the hog, the original owner of the soil, shall be penned up in a little reservation ten feet by twelve, made of cheap pine slabs.

Every principle of right, and justice, and equity, and humanity cries out against this tyrannical action on the part of the white man. Men who would scorn to do a dishonorable act, ordinarily, snatch the broad lands that were formerly owned by the hog, away from him, and deliberately go to raising wheat on them. This is not right. We should remember that the hog has certain rights which we are bound to respect.

Did you ever stop to think, dear reader, that the hog of the present day is but a poor, degraded specimen of the true aboriginal hog, before civilization had encroached upon him? Then do not join the popular cry against him. Once he was pure as the beautiful snow.

(*Bill Nye and Boomerang*, 1881)

Examining the Brand on a Frozen Steer

A stock owner went out the other day over the divide to see how his cattle were standing the rigorous weather, and found a large, fine steer in his last long sleep. The stockman had to roll him over to see the brand, and he has regretted his curiosity ever since. He told me that the brand looked to him like a Roman candle making almost 2,000 revolutions per moment, and with 187 more prismatic colors than he thought were in existence. Sometimes a steer is not dead but in a bold, sleepy stupor which precedes death, and when stirred up a little and irritated because he cannot die without turning over and showing his brand, he musters his remaining strength and kicks the inquisitive stockman so high that he can see and recognize the features of departed friends. That was the way it happened on this occasion. The stockman fell in the branches of a pine tree on Jack Creek, not dead but very thoughtful. He said he was near enough to hear the rush of wings, and was just going to register and engage a room in the New Jerusalem when he returned to consciousness.

(*Bill Nye and Boomerang*, 1881)

A Word About Wild Sheep

Scribner's Monthly has the following little fragment of information relative to western zoology, which we cheerfully reprint. Not so much on account of its novelty, but for the breezy style in which it is narrated:

"At the base of Sheep Rock, one of the winter strongholds of the Shasta flocks, there lives a stockraiser who has the advantage of observing the movements of wild sheep every winter; and in the course of a conversation with him on the subject of their diving habits, he pointed to the front of a lava headland about a hundred and fifty feet high, which is only eight or ten degrees out of the perpendicular. 'There,' said he, 'I followed a band of them fellows to the back of that rock yonder, and expected to capture them all, for I thought I had a dead thing on them. I got behind them on a narrow bench that runs along the face of the wall near the top, and comes to an end where they couldn't get away without falling and being killed; but they jumped off and landed all right as if that were the regular thing with them."

We don't wish to rub off the flush and bloom of this story, because we hate to have any one sit down on a favorite lie of ours, but there are little weak places in the above statement. For instance, a mountain sheep has bowels. He uses them in deducting the nutritious properties of the bunch grass and moss agates which he puts into his system. Examination by well known anatomists has shown, that the bowels of the mountain sheep are constructed on the old plan instead of being made of Bessemer steel, with copper rivets and dust-proof brass cap, as is generally supposed.

A fall of 150 feet perpendicularly would mix up the works of a mountain sheep so that he wouldn't know whether he had diphtheria or inflammation of the bowels.

Again, the mountain sheep, like all vertebrates, has a spinal column, something like the editorial column of this paper. The general impression that the backbone of a mountain sheep is made of vulcanized rubber and spiral springs is incorrect. If he were to jump 150 feet, therefore, toward the center of the earth, something would have to flummix.

The chances are that he would find his lumbar vertebrae in his vest pocket and his gambrel joint jammed through his liver. We do not deny that the mountain sheep has a forehead that is harder to drill a fact through than that of the average spring poet, but his forehead only protects his intellect. It don't prevent his hind legs jamming through his diaphragm when he jumps 150 feet, and strikes on a chunk of prehistoric granite.

We don't want to say anything disrespectful of *Scribner's Monthly*, because it is older than we are, and we want to be respectful to old age; but whenever you find a place where a flock of mountain sheep have jumped down a precipice 150 feet deep, you can go and gather up more giblets of wild mutton than you will use all summer.

(*Forty Liars, and Other Lies*, 1882)

About the Ostrich

There is some prospect of ostrich farming developing into quite an industry in the southwest, and it will sometime be a cold day when the simple-minded rustic of that region will not have ostrich on toast if he wants it. Ostrich farming, however, will always have its drawbacks. The hen ostrich is not a good layer as a rule, only laying two eggs per annum, which, being about the size of a porcelain wash bowl, make her so proud that she takes the balance of the year for the purpose of convalescing.

The ostrich is chiefly valuable for the plumage which he wears, and which, when introduced into the world of commerce, makes the husband almost wish that he were dead.

Probably the ostrich will not come into general use as an article of food, few people caring for it, as the meat is coarse, and the gizzard full of old hardware, and relics of wrecked trains and old irons left where there has been a fire.

Carving the ostrich is not so difficult as carving the quail, because the joints are larger and one can find them with less trouble. Still, the bird takes up a great deal of room at the table, and the best circles are not using them.

The ostrich does not set. She don't have time. She does not squat down over something and insist on hatching it out if it takes all summer, but she just lays a couple of porcelain cuspidors in the hot sand when she feels like it, and then goes away to the seaside to quiet her shattered nerves.

(*Baled Hay*, 1884)

Firmness

We were pained to see a large mule brought into town yesterday with his side worn away until it looked very thin. It looked as though the pensive mule had laid down to think over his past life, and being in the company of seven other able-bodied mules, all of whom were attached to a government freight wagon going down a mountain, this particular animal, while wrapped in a brown study, had been pulled several miles with so much unction, as it were, that when the train stopped it was found that this large and highly accomplished mule had worn his side off so thin that you could see his inmost thoughts.

When we saw him, he looked as though, if he had his life to live over again, he would select a different time to ponder over his previous history. Sometimes a mule's firmness causes his teetotal and everlasting overthrow.

Firmness is a good thing in its place, but we should early learn that to be firm we need not stand up against a cyclone till our eternal economy is blown into the tops of the neighboring trees. Moral courage is a good thing, but it is useless unless you have a liver to go along with it. Sometimes a man is required to lay down his life for his principles, but the cases where he is expected to lay down his digester on the altar of his belief, are comparatively seldom.

We may often learn a valuable lesson from the stubborn

mule, and guard against the too protuberant use of our own ideas in opposition to other powers against which it is useless to contend. It may be wrong for giant powder to blow the top of a man's head off without cause, but repeated contests have proved that even when giant powder is in the wrong, it is eventually victorious.

Let us, therefore, while reasonably fixed in our purpose, avoid the display of a degree of firmness which will scatter us around over two school districts, and confuse the coroner in his inquest.

(*Baled Hay*, 1884)

My Dog

I have owned quite a number of dogs in my life, but they are all dead now. Last evening I visited my dog cemetery—just between the gloaming and the shank of the evening. On the biscuit-box cover that stands at the head of a little mound fringed with golden rod and pickle bottles, the idler may still read these lines, etched in red chalk by a trembling hand:

Little Kosciusko,
———NOT DEAD,———
but jerked hence
By Request
S. Y. L.
(*See you Later.*)

I do not know why he was called Kosciusko. I do not care. I only know that his little grave stands out there while the gloaming gloams and the soughing winds are soughing.

Do you ask why I am alone here and dogless in this weary world?

I will tell you anyhow. It will not take long, and it may do me good.

Kosciusko came to me one night in winter with no baggage and unidentified. When I opened the door, he came in as though he had left something in there by mistake and had returned for it.

He stayed with us two years as a watch-dog. In a desultory way, he was a good watch-dog. If he had watched other people with the same unrelenting scrutiny with which he watched me, I might have felt his death more keenly than I do now.

The second year that little Kosciusko was with us I shaved off a full beard one day while down town, put on a clean collar and otherwise disguised myself intending to surprise my wife.

Kosciusko sat on the front porch when I returned. He looked at me as the cashier of a bank does when a newspaper man goes in to get a suspiciously large check cashed. He did not know me. I said, "Kosciusko, have you forgotten your master's voice?"

He smiled sarcastically, showing his glorious wealth of mouth, but still sat there as though he had stuck his tail into the door-steps and couldn't get it out.

So I waived the formality of going in at the front door, and went around to the portcullis, on the off side of the house, but Kosciusko was there when I arrived. The cook, seeing a stranger lurking around the manor house, encouraged Kosciusko to come and gorge himself with a part of my leg, which he did. Acting on this hint, I went to the barn. I do not know why I went to the barn, but somehow there was nothing in the house that I wanted. When a man wants to be by himself, there is no place like a good, quiet barn for thought. So I went into the barn, about three feet prior to Kosciusko.

Noticing the stairway, I ascended it in an aimless kind of way, about four steps at a time. What happened when we got into the haymow, I do not now recall, only that Kosciusko and I frolicked around there in the hay for some time. Occasionally I would be on top, and then he would have all the delegates, until finally I got hold of a pitch-fork, and freedom shrieked when Kosciusko fell. I wrapped myself up in an old horse-net and went into the house. Some of my clothes were afterward found in the hay, and the doctor pried a part of my person out of Kosciusko's jaws, but not enough to do me any good.

I have owned, in all, eleven dogs, and they all died violent deaths and went out of the world totally unprepared to die.

(*Bill Nye's Remarks*, 1887)

A Goat in a Frame

Laramie has a seal brown goat, with iron gray chin whiskers and a breath like new mown hay.

He has not had as hard a winter as the majority of stock on the Rocky Mountains because he is of a domestic turn of mind and tries to make man his friend. Though social in his nature, he never intrudes himself on people after they have intimated with a shotgun that they are weary of him.

When the world seems cold and dark to him, and everybody turns coldly away from him, he does not steal away by himself and die of corroding grief; he just lies down on the sidewalk in the sun and fills the air with the seductive fragrance of which he is the sole proprietor.

One day, just as he had eaten his midday meal of boot heels and cold sliced atmosphere and kerosene barrel staves, he saw a man going along the street with a large looking glass under his arm.

The goat watched the man, and saw him set the mirror down by a gate and go inside the house after some more things that he was moving. Then the goat stammered with his tail a few times and went up to see if he could eat the mirror.

When he got pretty close to it, he saw a hungry-looking goat apparently coming toward him, so he backed off a few yards and went for him. There was a loud crash, and when the man came out he saw a full length portrait of a goat with a heavy, black walnut frame around it going down the street with a great deal of apparent relish.

Then the man said something derogatory about the goat, and seemed offended about something.

Goats are not timid in their nature and are easily domesticated.

There are two kinds of goat—the cashmere goat and the plain goat. The former is worked up into cashmere shawls and cashmere bouquet. The latter is not.

The cashmere bouquet of commerce is not made of the common goat. It is a good thing that it is not.

A goat that has always been treated with uniform kindness and never betrayed may be taught to eat out of the hand. Also out of the flour barrel or the ice cream freezer.

(*Bill Nye's Remarks*, 1887)

A Discourse on Cats

I am not fond of cats as a general rule. I never yearned to have one around the house. My idea always was that I could have trouble enough in a legitimate way without adding a cat to my woes. With a belligerent cook and a communistic laundress, it seems to me most anybody ought to be unhappy enough without a cat.

I never owned one until a tramp cat came to our house one day during the present autumn—and tearfully asked to be loved. He didn't have anything in his make-up that was calculated to win anybody's love, but he seemed contented with a little affection—one ear was gone, and his tail was bald for six inches at the end, and he was otherwise well calculated to win confidence and sympathy. Though we could not be madly in love with him, we decided to be friends, and give him a chance to win the general respect.

Everything would have turned out all right if the bobtail waif had not been a little given to investigation. He wanted to know more about the great world in which he lived, so he began by inspecting my house. He got into the store-room closet, and found a place where the carpenter had not completed his job. This is a feature of the Laramie artisan's style. He leaves little places in unobserved corners generally, so that he can come back some day and finish it at an additional cost of fifty dollars. This cat observed that he could enter at this point and go all over the imposing structure between the flooring and the ceiling. He proceeded to do so.

* * *

We will now suppose that a period of two days has passed. The wide halls and spacious *facades* of the Nye mansion are still. The lights in the banquet-hall are extinguished, and the ice-cream freezer is hushed to rest in the woodshed. A soft and tearful yowl, deepened into a regular ring-tail-peeler, spits the solemn night in twain. Nobody seemed to know where it came from. I rose softly and went to where the sound had seemed to well up from. It was not there.

I stood on a piece of cracker in the dining-room a moment, waiting for it to come again. This time it came from the boudoir of our French artist in soup-bone symphonies and pie—Mademoiselle Bridget O'Dooley. I went there and opened the door softly, so as to let the cat out without disturbing the giant mind that had worn itself out during the day in the kitchen, bestowing a dry shampoo to the china.

Then I changed my mind and came out. Several articles of *vertu*, beside Bridget, followed me with some degree of vigor.

The next time the tramp cat yowled he seemed to be in the recesses of the bathroom, I went downstairs and investigated. In doing so I drove my superior toe into my foot, out of sight, with a door that I encountered. My wife joined me in the search. She could not do much, but she aided me a thousand times by her counsel. If it had not been for her mature advice I might have lost much of the invigorating exercise of that memorable night.

Toward morning we discovered that the cat was between the floor of the children's play-room and the ceiling of the dining-room. We tried till daylight to persuade the cat to come out and get acquainted, but he would not.

At last we decided that the quickest way to get the poor little thing out was to let him die in there, and then we could tear up that portion of the house and get him out. While he lived we couldn't keep him still long enough to tear a hole in the house and get at him.

It was a little unpleasant for a day or two waiting for death to come to his relief, for he seemed to die hard, but at last the unearthly midnight yowl was still. The plaintive little voice ceased to vibrate on the still and pulseless air. Later, we found, however, that he was not dead. In a lucid interval he had discovered the hole in the store-room where he entered, and, as we found afterward a gallon of coal-oil spilled in a barrel of cut-loaf sugar, we concluded that he had escaped by that route.

That was the only time that I ever kept a cat, and I didn't do it then because I was suffering for something to fondle. I've got a good deal of surplus affection, I know, but I don't have to spread it out over a stump-tail orphan cat.

(*Bill Nye's Chestnuts, Old and New*, 1889)

How to Hunt the Fox

The joyous season for hunting is again upon us, and with the gentle fall of the autumn leaf and the sough of the scented breezes about the gnarled and naked limbs of the wailing trees—the huntsman comes with his hark and his halloo and hurrah, boys, the swift rush of the chase, the thrilling scamper 'cross country, the mad dash through the Long Islander's pumpkin patch—also the mad dash, dash, dash of the farmer, the low moan of the disabled and frozen-toed hen as the whooping horsemen run her down; the wild shriek of the children, the low melancholy wail of the frightened shoat as he flees away to the straw pile, the quick yet muffled plunk of the frozen tomato and the dull scrunch of the seed cucumber.

The huntsman now takes the flannels off his fox, rubs his stiffened limbs with gargling oil, ties a bunch of firecrackers to his tail and runs him around the barn a few times to see if he is in good order.

The foxhound is a cross of the bloodhound, the grayhound, the bulldog and the chump. When you step on his tail he is said to be in full cry. The foxhound obtains from his ancestors on the bloodhound side of the house his keen scent, which enables him while in full cry 'cross country to pause and hunt for chipmunks. He also obtains from the bloodhound branch of his family a wild yearning to star in an "Uncle Tom" company, and watch little Eva meander up the flume at two dollars per week. From the grayhound he gets his most miraculous speed, which enables him to attain a rate of velocity so great that he is unable to halt during the excitement of the chase, frequently running so far during the day that it takes him a week to get back, when, of course, all interest has died out. From the bulldog the foxhound obtains his great tenacity of purpose, his deep-seated convictions, his quick perceptions, his love of home and his clinging nature. From the chump the foxhound gets his high intellectuality and that mental power which enables him to distinguish almost at a glance the salient points of difference between a two-year-old steer and a two-dollar bill.

The foxhound is about two feet in height, and 120 of them would be considered an ample number for a quiet little fox hunt. Some hunters think this number inadequate, but unless the fox be unusually skittish and crawl under the barn, 120 foxhounds ought to be enough. The trouble generally is that hunters make too much noise, thus scaring the fox so that he tries to get away from them. This necessitates hard riding and great activity on the part of the whippers-in. Frightening a fox almost always results in sending him out of the road and compelling horsemen to stop in order to take down a panel of fence every little while that they may follow the animal, and before you can get the fence put up again the owner is on the ground, and after you have made change with him and mounted again the fox may be nine miles away. Try by all means to keep your fox in the road!

It makes a great difference what kind of fox you use, however. I once had a fox on my Pumpkin Butte estates that lasted me three years, and I never knew him to shy or turn out of the road for anything but a loaded team. He was the best fox for hunting purposes that I ever had. Every spring I would sprinkle him with Scotch snuff and put him away in the bureau till fall. He would then come out bright and chipper. He was always ready to enter into the chase with all the chic and embonpoint of a regular Kenosha, and nothing pleased him better than to be about eight miles in advance of my thoroughbred pack in full cry, scampering 'cross country, while stretching back a few miles behind the dogs followed a pale young man and his fiancier, each riding a horse that had sat down too hard on its tail some time and driven it into his system about six joints.

Some hunters, who are madly and passionately devoted to the sport, leap their horses over fences, moats, donjon keeps, hedges and currant bushes with utter sang froid and the wild, unfettered toot ongsomble of a brass band. It is one of the most spirited and touchful of sights to see a young fox-hunter going home through the gloaming with a full cry in one hand and his pancreas in the other.

Some like to be in at the death, as it is called, and it is certainly a laudable ambition. To see 120 dogs hold out against a ferocious fox weighing nine pounds; to watch the brave little band of dogs and whippers-in and horses with sawed-off tails, making up in heroism what they lack in numbers, succeeding at last in ridding the country of the ferocious brute which has long been the acknowledged foe of the human race, is indeed a fine sight.

We are too apt to regard fox-hunting merely as a relaxation, a source of pleasure, and the result of a desire to do the way people do in the novels which we steal from English authors; but this is not all. To successfully hunt a fox, to jump fences 'cross country like an unruly steer, is no child's play. To ride all day on a very hot and restless saddle, trying to lope while your horse is trotting, giving your friends a good view of the country between yourself and your horse, then leaping stone walls, breaking your collar-bone in four places, pulling out one eye and leaving it hanging on a plum tree, or going home at night with your transverse colon wrapped around the pommel of your saddle and your liver in an old newspaper, requires the greatest courage.

Too much stress cannot be placed upon the costume worn while fox-hunting, and in fact, that is, after all, the life and soul of the chase. For ladies, nothing looks better than a close-fitting jacket, sewed together with thread of the same shade and a skirt. Neat-fitting cavalry boots and a plug hat complete the costume. Then, with a hue in one hand and a cry in the other, she is prepared to mount. Lead the horse up to a stone wall or a freight car and spring lightly into the saddle with a glad cry. A freight car is the best thing from which to mount a horse, but it is too unwieldy and frequently delays the chase. For this reason, too, much luggage should not be carried on a fox-hunt. Some gentlemen carry a change of canes, neatly concealed in a shawl strap, but even this may be dispensed with.

For gentlemen, a dark, four-button cutaway coat, with neat, loose-fitting, white panties, will generally scare a fox into convulsions, so that he may be easily killed with a club. A short-waisted plug hat may be worn also, in order to distinguish the hunter from the whipper-in, who wears a baseball cap. The only fox-hunting I have ever done was on board an impetuous, tough-bitted, fore-and-aft horse that had emotional insanity. I was dressed in a swallow-tail coat, waistcoat of Scotch plaid Turkish toweling, and a pair of close-fitting breeches of etiquette tucked into my boot-tops. As I was away from home at the time and could not reach my own steed I was obliged to mount a spirited steed with high, intellectual hips, one white eye and a big red nostril that you could set a Shanghai hen in. This horse, as soon as the pack broke into full cry, climbed over a fence that had wrought-iron briers on it, lit in a corn field, stabbed his hind leg through a sere and yellow pumpkin, which he wore the rest of the day, with seven yards of pumpkin vine streaming out of behind, and away we dashed 'cross country. I remained mounted not because I enjoyed it, for I did not, but because I dreaded to dismount. I hated to get off in pieces. If I can't get off a horse's back as a whole, I would rather adhere to the horse. I will adhere that I did so.

We did not see the fox, but we saw almost everything else. I remember, among other things, of riding through a hothouse and how I enjoyed it. A morning scamper through a conservatory when the syringas and jonquils and jack roses lie cuddled up together in their little beds, is a thing to remember and look back to and pay for. To stand knee-deep in glass and gladiolas, to smell the mashed and mussed up mignonette and the last fragrant sigh of the scrunched heliotrope beneath the hoof of your horse, while far away the deep-mouthed baying of the hoarse hounds, hotly hugging the reeking trail of the anise-seed bag, calls on the gorgeously caparisoned hills to give back their merry music or fork it over to other answering hills, is joy to the huntsman's heart.

On, on I rode with my unconfined locks streaming behind me in the autumn wind. On and still on I sped, the big, bright pumpkin slipping up and down the gambrel of my spirited horse at every jump. On and ever on we went, shedding terror and pumpkin seeds along our glittering track till my proud steed ran his leg in a gopher hole and fell over one of those machines that they put on a high-headed steer to keep him from jumping fences. As the horse fell, the necklace of this hickory poke flew up and adjusted itself around my throat. In an instant my steed was on his feet again, and gayly we went forward while the prong of this barbarous appliance, ever and anon plowed into a brand new culvert or rooted up a clover field. Every time it ran into an orchard or a cemetery it would jar my neck and knock me silly. But I could see with joy that it reduced the speed of my horse. At last as the sun went down, reluctantly, it seemed to me, for he knew that he would never see such riding again, my ill-spent horse fell with a hollow moan, curled up, gave a spasmodic quiver with his little, nerveless, sawed-off tail and died.

The other huntsmen succeeded in treeing the anise-seed bag at sundown, in time to catch the 6 o'clock train home.

Fox-hunting is one of the most thrilling pastimes of which I know, and for young men whose parents have amassed large sums of money in the intellectual pursuit of hides and tallow, the meet, the chase, the scamper, the full cry, the cover, the stellated fracture, the yelp of the pack, the yip, the yell of triumph, the confusion, the whoop, the holla, the hallos, the hurrah, the abrasion, the snort of the hunter, the concussion, the sward, the open, the earth stopper, the strangulated hernia, the glad cry of the hound as he brings home the quivering seat of the peasant's pantaloons, the yelp of joy as he lays at his master's feet, the strawberry mark of the rustic, all, all are exhilarating to the sons of our American nobility.

Fox-hunting combines the danger and the wild, tumultuous joy of the skating-rink, the toboggan slide, the mush-and-milk sociable and the straw ride.

With a good horse, an air cushion, a reliable earth-stopper and an anise-seed bag, a man must indeed be thoroughly blase who can not enjoy a scamper across country, over the Pennsylvania wold, the New Jersey mere, the Connecticut moor, the Indiana glade, the Missouri brake, the Michigan mead, the American tarn, the fen, the gulch, the buffalo wallow, the cranberry marsh, the glen, the draw, the canyon, the ravine, the forks, the bottom or the settlement.

For the young American nobleman whose ducal father made his money by inventing a fluent pill, or who gained his great wealth through relieving humanity by means of a lung pad, a liver pad, a kidney pad or a foot pad, fox-hunting is first-rate.

(*Nye and Riley's Railway Guide*, 1888)

CHAPTER 3

Imperfect Sympathies

Concerning Coroners

I am glad to notice that in the East there is a growing disfavor in the public mind for selecting a practicing physician for the office of coroner. This matter should have attracted attention years ago. Now it gratifies me to notice a finer feeling on the part of the people, and an awakening of those sensibilities which go to make life more highly prized and far more enjoyable.

I had the misfortune at one time to be under the medical charge of a coroner who had graduated from a Chicago morgue and practiced medicine along with his inquest business with the most fiendish delight. I do not know which he enjoyed best, holding the inquest or practicing on his patient and getting the victim ready for the quest.

One day he wrote out a prescription and left it for me to have filled. I was surprised to find that he had made a mistake and left a rough draft of the verdict in my own case and a list of jurors which he had made in memorandum so as to be ready for the worst. I was alarmed, for I did not know that I was in so dangerous a condition. He had the advantage of me, for he knew just what he was giving me, and how long human life could be sustained under his treatment. I did not.

That is why I say that the profession of medicine should

not be allowed to conflict with the solemn duties of the coroner. They are constantly clashing and infringing upon each other's territory. This coroner had a kind of tread-softly-bow-the-head way of getting around the room that made my flesh creep. He had a way, too, when I was asleep, of glancing hurriedly through the pockets of my pantaloons as they hung over a chair, probably to see what evidence he could find that might aid the jury in arriving at a verdict. Once I woke up and found him examining a draft that he had found in my pocket. I asked him what he was doing with my funds, and he said that he thought he detected a draft in the room and he had just found out where it came from.

After that I hoped that death would come to my relief as speedily as possible. I felt that death would be a happy release from the cold touch of the amateur coroner and pro tem physician. I could look forward with pleasure, and even joy, to the moment when my physician would come for the last time in his professional capacity and go to work on me officially. Then the county would be obliged to pay him, and the undertaker could take charge of the fragments left by the inquest.

The duties of the physician are with the living, those of the coroner with the dead. No effort, therefore, should be made to unite them. It is in violation of all the finer feelings of humanity. When the physician decides that his tendencies point mostly toward immortality and the names of his patients are nearly all found on the moss-covered stones of the cemetery, he may abandon the profession with safety and take hold of politics. Then, should his tastes lead him to the inquest, let him gravitate toward the office of coroner; but the two should not be united.

No man ought to follow his fellow down the mysterious river that defines the boundary between the known and the unknown, and charge him professionally till his soul has fled and then charge a per diem to the county for prying into his internal economy and holding an inquest over the debris of mortality. I therefore hail this movement with joy and wish to encourage it in every way. It points toward a degree of enlightenment which will be in strong contrast with the darker and more ignorant epochs of time, when the practice of medicine was united with the profession of the barber, the well-digger, the farrier, the veterinarian or the coroner.

Why, this physician plenipotentiary and coroner extraordinary that I have referred to didn't know when he got a call whether to take his morphine syringe or his venire for a jury. He very frequently went to see a patient with a lung tester under one arm and the revised statutes under the other. People never knew when they saw him going to a neighbor's house whether the case had yielded to the coroner's treatment or not. No one ever knew just when over-taxed nature would yield to the statutes in such case made and provided.

When the jury was impanelled, however, we always knew that the medical treatment had been successful fatal.

Once he charged the county with an inquest he felt sure of, but in the night the patient got delirious, eluded his nurse, the physician and coroner, and fled to the foothills, where he was taken care of and finally recovered. The experiences of some of the patients who escaped from this man read more like fiction than fact. One man revived during the inquest, knocked the foreman of the jury through the window, kicked the coroner in the stomach, fed him a bottle of violet ink, and, with a shriek of laughter, fled. He is now traveling under an assumed name with a mammoth circus, feeding his bald head to the African lion twice a day at $9 a week and found.

(*Bill Nye's Remarks*, 1887)

Gingerbread Poems and Cold Pickled Facts

In an old number of *Harper's Magazine* will be found a little poem upon the subject of Joseph, the chief of the Nez Perces. There is a kind of mellow and subdued heroic light cast over the final defeat of this great North American horse thief, which is in perfectly pleasing harmony with the New England idea of the noble unfettered relic of a defunct race. This soft-voiced poet, who probably knows about as much of the true occidental pig-stealer as the latter does about the Electoral College, starts out this little brass-mounted epic in the following elegant style of prevarication:

> From the northern desolation,
> Comes the cry of exultation,
> It has ended—he has yielded, and the stubborn fight is won.
> Let the nation in its glory,
> Bow with shame before the story
> Of the hero it has ruined, and the evil it has done.

It is too true that here in the wild West people haven't the advantages that are accorded to the East, and in our uncouth ignorance, and meager facilities for obtaining information, we are, no doubt, too prone to ascribe to the hostile inebriate of the plains a character which does not compare very favorably with the boss hero in the poem hereto attached and marked "Exhibit A." But the people on the frontier should not set themselves up to judge what they know nothing of. Why should frontiersmen, without colleges, without observatories, without telescopes, or logarithms, or protoplasms, or spectroscopes, or heliotropes, how should they, I ask, who can lay no claim to anything but that they are poor, unsophisticated, grasshopper sufferers; with nothing to refer to but the naked facts—the ruins of their desolated homes, and the ghastly, mutilated corpses of their wives and children—try to compete with the venerable philosophers who live where the Patent Office reports are made, and within the shadow of the building in which the *Illustrated Police Gazette* and other such reliable authorities have their birth, and in which are illustrated with graphic skill the Indian raids of the border, using the same old cut which is taken from the "Death of Captain Cook" to illustrate every Indian outbreak from Nebraska to Oregon.

Is it nothing forsooth for a nomadic race of buffalo slayers and maple sugar makers and cranberry pickers to rise from the dust and learn to love the wise institutions of a free government? To lay aside the old hickory bow of the original red man and take up the improved breech-loader? To take kindly to mixed drinks and Sabbath school picnics and temperance lectures and baseball matches? To live contentedly about the agencies, playing poker for the whiskies during the cold and cruel winter? Then when the glad song of the robin awakes the echoes in spring, and the air is filled with a thousand nameless odors, among which may be detected the balmy breath of the government sock, to hie him away to the valleys with his fishing rod and flies (and other curious insects), or to spend the glorious days of midsummer at the camp meeting or the horse race? We can never know how his poor heart must burn to kick off his box-toed boots and throw aside his dress coat and suspenders, and gallop over the green hills and kick up his heels and whoop and yell, and tear out the tongues of a few white women and be sociable.

They are indeed the nation's wards, a little frisky and playful at times, to be sure, but we must overlook that. There can be no reason nor justice in forbidding these freeborn descendants of these mighty races the inalienable right to lock up their front doors at the agency and put the key in their pockets, and light out, if they wish to, across the country, spreading gory desolation along their trail, eating the farmers' hard earned store, pillaging his home, murdering his household, burning his crops, riding their war horses over his watermelon vines, eating his winter preserves, scalping the hired man and wearing away the farmer's red-flannel undershirt wrong side to, and wrong side up if they want to. And if any ignorant upstart of the frontier, who feels a little sore over the loss of his family, undertakes to defraud these wild, free sons of the forest of any or all of their rights, let the lop-eared, slab-sided, knock-kneed, cross-eyed, spavined, lantern-jawed, sway-backed, mangy, flannel-mouthed poet of the educated and refined East write poetry about him till he is glad to apologize.

(*Bill Nye and Boomerang*, 1881)

Home-Made Indian Relics

Sherman, on the Union Pacific Railroad, is the loftiest by a considerable majority of any point on the road. This fact has occasioned some little notoriety for Sherman, and on the strength of it a small reservoir of Western curiosities has been established there.

I went over to the curiosity ranche while the train was taking breath, to see what I could see and buy it if the price were not too high.

There were a great many Western curiosities from various parts of the country, and I got deeply interested in them.

I love to find some old relic of ancient times or some antique weapon of warfare peculiar to the noble Aztecs. I can ponder over them by the hour and enjoy it first rate.

Among the living wonders I noticed a bale of Indian arrows. These arrows are beautiful to look upon, and are remarkably well preserved. They are as good as new. I asked, simply as a matter of form, if they were Indian arrows. The man said they were. Then I asked who made them, and he got mad and wouldn't speak to me.

I do not think I am unreasonable to want to know who makes my Indian arrows, am I?

I am willing to pay a fair price for the genuine Connecticut made arrow with cane shaft and warranted cast steel point, but the Indian arrow made at Omaha is not durable.

This curiosity man would make more money and command a larger trade if he were not so quick-tempered.

He had also some Western cactus as a curiosity for the tenderfoot who had never fooled with a cactus much.

It was the clear thing, however. I sat down on one to test its genuineness. It stood the test better than I did. When you have doubts about a cactus and don't know whether it is a genuine cactus or a young watermelon with its hair banged, you can test it by sitting down on it. It may surprise you at first, but it tickles the cactus almost to death.

For a high-priced house plant and gentle meek-eyed exotic that don't care much for affection, the Rocky Mountain cactus takes the cake.

It is very easy to live, and don't require much fondling. It will enjoy life better if you will get mad at it about once a week and pull it up by the roots and kick it around the yard. Water it carefully every four years; if you water it oftener than that, it will be surprised, and gradually pine away and die.

Another item I must not forget in giving directions for the cultivation of this rare tropical plant: get some one to sit down on it occasionally—if you don't feel equal to it yourself. There's nothing that makes a cactus thrive and flourish so much as to have a victim with linen pants on, sit down on it and then get up impulsively like. If a cactus can have these little attentions bestowed upon it, it will live to a good old age, and insinuate itself through the pantaloons of generations yet unborn. Plant in a gravelly, coarse soil, and kick it every time you think of it.

Returning to our subject, however, I think the Indian is a trifle uncertain and at times tricky by nature. Of course I do not wish to say anything that would have a tendency to injure the reputation of the Indian, for in all candor I will say that he means well.

I do not wish to have what I may say published as coming from me, because the Indian has always used me well, perhaps because I never allow myself to stray into his jurisdiction, but he has little, hateful, mean ways which I despise. Some think that if he were to have more chance to learn, more normal schools and baseball clubs and upright pianos, he would have more ambition to do right and get ahead, but I almost doubt it.

I am very humane myself, but I am more apt to be harsh in my measures with the Indian than most Eastern people of culture are. Perhaps this is because I have seen people who had been shot full of large size bullet holes by the red man. This makes a difference, and I may be prejudiced.

When the average philanthropist has seen a family lying scattered around promiscuous and shot so full of holes that even the coarsest kind of food is of no use, he begins to ask in his mind whether a more severe method of treatment would not be beneficial to the Indian.

I want to look this matter calmly in the face, and ask whether night shirts and civilization and suspenders will make good citizens out of these unfettered children of the forest or not? Is it the opinion of the gentle reader that a nation of flea-bitten, smoke-tanned beggars will come forward and submit to the ennobling influences of Christianity and duck vests and horseshoe scarf pins and quarterly meetings and gauze underwear? Methinks not.

Nature constructed the noble red man with certain little mental, moral and physical eccentricities, and these eccentricities can be better worn away and remodeled on the evergreen shore.

Poor, weak, fallible man cannot successfully grapple with the task of working over an entire nation of human beings and changing the whole trend, so to speak, of a nation's mental and moral nature.

Let us not, therefore, usurp the prerogative or attempt to perform the Herculean task which a wise Creator has laid out for Himself.

The policy of Divine administration, if I mistake not, is

to improve the Indian and reform him in a future state in a large corral where the worm dieth not. This of course is only my private opinion, and I am offering it now in packages containing six each, securely boxed and sent free to any address on receipt of $1. I would sell it cheaper were it not for the excessive freight and the recent rise in white paper.

Supposing then the above to be the correct theory, what can poor erring man do to forward the good work? Evidently he can do nothing unless it be to change the state of the red man from a discouraging and annoying mortality to a bright and shining immortality.

I would suggest that this be done so far as possible by those who can spare the time and ammunition to do so. I will give to such all the encouragement and moral support I can. I would assist in the good work, but I am most too busy now planting my raspberry jam and setting out my early Swedish dried apple pie plant.

(*Bill Nye and Boomerang*, 1881)

The Annual Wail

As usual, the regular fall wail of the eastern press on the Indian question, charging that the Indians never committed any depredations unless grossly abused, has arrived. We are unpacking it this morning and marking the price on it. Some of it is on manifold, and the remainder on ordinary telegraph paper. It will be closed out very cheap. Parties wishing to supply boarding schools with essays and compositions, cannot do better than to apply at once. We are selling Boston lots, with large brass-mounted words, at two and three cents per pound. Every package draws a prize of a two-pound can of baked beans. If large orders are received from any one person, we will set up the wail and start it to running, free of cost. It may be attached to any newspaper in a few minutes, and the merest child can readily understand it. It is very simple. But it is not as simple as the tallowy poultice on the average eastern paper, who grinds them out at $4 per week, and found.

We also have some old wails, two or three years old—and older—that have never been used, which we will sell very low. Old Sioux wails, Modoc wails, etc., etc. They do not seem to meet with a ready sale in the west, and we rather suspect it's because we are too near the scene of the Indian troubles. Parties who have been shot at, scalped, or had their wives and children massacred by the Indians, do not buy eastern wails.

Eastern wails are meant for the eastern market, and if we can get this old stock off our hands, we will hereafter treat the Indian question in our plain, matter of fact way.

The namby-pamby style of Indian editorial and molasses-candy-gush that New Englanders are now taking in, makes us tired. Life is too short. It is but a span. Only as a tale that has been told. Just like the coming of a guest, who gets his meal ticket punched, grabs a tooth pick, and skins out.

Then why do we fool away the golden years that the Creator has given us for mental improvement and spiritual elevation, in trying to fill up the enlightened masses with an inferior article of taffy?

Every man who knows enough to feed himself out of a maple trough, knows, or ought to know, that the Indian is treacherous, dishonest, diabolical and devilish in the extreme, and that he is only waiting the opportunity to spread out a little juvenile hell over the fair face of nature if you give him one-sixteenth of a chance. He will wear pants and comb his hair, and pray and be a class leader at the agency for fifty-nine years, if he knows that in the summer of the sixtieth year he can murder a few Colorado settlers and beat out the brains of the industrious farmers.

Industry is the foe of the red man. He is a warrior. He has royal blood in his veins, and the vermin of the Montezumas dance the German over his filthy carcass. That's the kind of a hair pin he is. He never works. Nobody but Chinamen and plebeians ever work.

(*Baled Hay*, 1884)

Too Much God and No Flour

Old Chief Pocotello, now at the Fort Hall agency, in answer to an inquiry relative to the true Christian character of a former Indian agent at that place, gave in very terse language the most accurate description of a hypocrite that was ever given to the public. "Ugh! Too much God and no flour."

(*Baled Hay*, 1884)

The Mormons

The first installment of imported Mormons passed through here yesterday on its way to Zion. To all appearances, the stock of nihilists and foreign vagabonds is considerably reduced, and this year the prevailing style of imported Mormon will be the trichina impregnated variety left over from last year's round-up. Those who passed through yesterday were in a damaged condition, and nothing but the pure bracing air of the Jordan and a liberal dose of saltpetre can get them through the summer.

When they got here their trainer took the hose and turned it on the cages to purify the air a little, and then he let some of the more docile ones out for exercise, but there were some women in the rear car that the railroad authorities would not allow at large for fear they would scare the engines off the track.

One type of the proselyte Mormon is a man with three overcoats, and a pair of wooden shoes on, and a woolen lap-robe tied in a jaunty style around his neck. Most of them are afraid they will take cold. Their fears about taking a bath seem to be equally noticeable.

Bigamy, trigamy or polygamy can have no repulsive features for such people. Judging from their appearance, no horror could shock them unless it be a chunk of Castile soap and fresh air.

It is said that Mormonism is an abnormal growth upon our free institutions. This is true. It is a fungus growth like the toadstool above the ruin of an old hen ranch. It rises into the sunlight of freedom and towers toward the clear blue sky like a sore toe in a gale of wind.

It attaches itself to the life-giving institutions of America and hangs upon it like a freckle on the brow of beauty or an egg dado on a white vest.

We boast of the rights of free-born American citizens, and yet we allow the old dead horse of Mormonism to lie around among our young and growing territories till the pioneers of civilization have to wear patent clothes pins on their noses all summer while they make the desert bloom like the roses.

We don't want to seem at all officious or dictatorial just because we wield the mighty civilizing ball club of the press, but we would like to suggest that so long as polygamy and other forms of legalized prostitution are given the cushioned seats on the frontier, and impecunious white men with only one wife have to stand around and enjoy the show from the peanut gallery, the drawbacks of opening up a new country are too noticeable, and too contiguous.

(*Forty Liars, and Other Lies*, 1882)

The Revelation Racket in Utah

Our esteemed and extremely connubial contemporary, the *Deseret News*, says in a recent editorial:

"The Latter day Saints will rejoice to learn that the vacancies which have existed in the quorums of the twelve apostles and the first seven presidents of seventies are now filled. During the conference recently held, Elder Abram H. Cannon was unanimously chosen to be one of the first seven presidents of seventies, and he was ordained to that office on Monday, October 9th. Subsequently, the Lord, by revelation through His servant, Prest. John Taylor, designated by name, Brothers George Teasdale and Heber J. Grant, to be ordained to the apostleship, and Brother Seymour B. Young to fill the remaining vacancy in the presidency of the seventies. These brethren were ordained on Monday, October 16th, the two apostles under the hands of the first presidency and twelve, and the other under the hands of the twelve and the presidency of the seventies."

Now, that's a convenient system of politics and civil service. When there is a vacancy, the president, John Taylor, goes into his closet and has a revelation which settles it all right. If the man appointed vicariously by the Lord is not in every way satisfactory, he may be discharged by the same process. Instead, therefore, of being required to rally a large force of his friends to aid him in getting an appointment, the aspirant arranges solely with the party who runs the revelation business. It will be seen at a glance, therefore, that the man who can get the job of revelating in Zion has it pretty much his own way. We would not care who made the laws of Utah if we could do its revelating at so much per revelate.

Think of the power it gives a man in a community of blind believers. Imagine, if you please, the glorious possibilities in store for the man who can successfully reveal the word of the Lord in an easy, extemporaneous manner on five minutes notice.

This prerogative does not confine itself to politics alone. The impromptu revelator of the Jordan has revelations when he wants to evade the payment of a bill. He gets a divine order also if he desires to marry a beautiful maid or seal the new school ma'am to himself. He has a leverage which he can bring to bear upon the people of his diocese at all times, even more potent than the press, and it does not possess the drawbacks that a newspaper does. You can run an aggressive paper if you want to in this country, and up to the time of the funeral you have a pretty active and enjoyable time, but after the grave has been filled up with the clods of the valley and your widow has drawn her insurance, you naturally ask, "What is the advantage to be gained by this fearless style of journalism?"

Still, even the inspired racket has its drawbacks. Last year, a little incident occurred in a Mormon family down in southern Utah, which weighed about nine pounds, and when the *ex officio* husband, who had been absent two years, returned, he acted kind of wild and surprised, somehow, and as he went through the daily round of his work he could be seen counting his fingers back and forth and looking at the almanac, and adding up little amounts on the side of the barn with a piece of red chalk.

Finally, one of the inspired mob of that part of the vineyard thought it was about time to get a revelation and go down there, so he did so. He sailed up to the *de facto* husband and *quasi* parent and solemnly straightened up some little irregularities as to dates, but the revelation was received with disdain, and the revelator was sent home in an old ore sack and buried in a peach basket.

Sometimes there is, even in Utah, a manifestation of such irreverence and open hostility to the church that it makes us shudder.

(*Baled Hay*, 1884)

Murray and the Mormons

Gov. Murray, the gritty Gentile governor of Utah, would be noticed in a crowd. He is very tall, yet well proportioned, square-built and handsome. He was called fine-looking in Kentucky, but the narrow-chested apostle of the abnormally connubial creed does not see anything pretty about him. Murray moves about through Salt Lake City in a cool, self-possessed kind of way that is very annoying to the church. Full-bearded, with brown moustache and dark hair parted a little to leeward of center, clothed in a diagonal Prince Albert coat, a silk hat and other clothes, he strolls through Zion like a man who hasn't got a yelping majority of ignorant lepers, led by a remorseless gang of nickel-plated apostles, thirsting for his young blood. I really believe he don't care a continental. The days of the avenging angel and the meek-eyed Danite, carrying a large sock loaded with buckshot, are over, perhaps; but only those who try to be Gentiles in a land of polygamous wives and anonymous white-eyed children, know how very unpopular it is. Judge Goodwin, of the Tribune, feels lonesome if he gets through the day without a poorly spelled, spattered, daubed and profane valentine threatening his life. The last time I saw him he showed me a few of them. They generally referred to him as a blankety blank "skunk" and a "hound of hell." He said he hoped I would pardon him for the apparent egotism, but he felt as though the Tribune was attracting attention almost every day. Some of these little billet-doux invited him to call at a trysting place on Tribune avenue and get his alleged brains scattered over a vacant lot. Most all of them threatened him with a rectangular head, a tin ear, or a watch pocket under the eye. He didn't seem to care much. He felt pleased and proud. Goodwin was always pleased with things that other men didn't like much. In the old days, when he and Mark Twain and Dan DeQuille were together, this was noticed in him.

Gov. Murray is the same way. He feels the public pulse, and says to himself: "Sometime there's going to be music here by the entire band, and I desire to be where I shan't miss a note."

There are people who think the Mormons will not fight. Perhaps not. They won't if they are let alone and allowed to fill the sage brush and line the banks of the Jordan with juvenile *nom de plumes*. They are peaceful while they may populate Utah and invade adjoining territories with their herds of ostensible wives and prattling progeny; while they can bring in every year via Castle Garden and the stock yards palace emigrant car, thousands of proselyted paupers from every pest house of Europe, and the free-love idiots of America. But when Murray gets an act of congress at his back and a squad of nervy, gamy, law-abiding monogamous assistants appointed by the president under that act of congress to knock crosswise and crooked the Jim Crow revelations of Utah and Mormondom, you will see the fur fly, and the fragrant follower of a false prophet will rise up William Riley and the regular army will feel lonesome. I asked a staff officer in one of the territories last sumemr what would be the result if the Mormons, with their home drill and their arms and their devotion to home and their fraudulent religion, should awake Nicodemas and begin to massacre the Gentiles, and the regular army should be sent over the Wasatch range to quell the trouble.

"Why," said he, "the white-eyed followers of Mormonism would kill the regular army with clubs. You can wear out a tribe of hostile Indians when the grass gives out and the antelope hunts the foothills, but the Mormons make everything they eat, drink and wear. They don't care whether there's tariff or free trade. They can make everything from gunpowder to a knit undershirt, from a $250 revelation to a hand-made cocktail. When a church gets where it can make such cooking whisky as the Mormons do, it is time to call for volunteers and put down the hydra-headed monster."

If congress don't step on a technicality and fall down, it

looks like amusement ahead, and if a District of Columbia rule, or martial law, or tocsin of war is the result, Gov. Murray is a good style of war governor. He isn't the kind of a man to put on his wife's gossamer cloak and meander over into Montana. He would give the matter his attention, and you would find him in the neighborhood when the national government decided to sit down on disorderly conduct in Utah. The first lever to be used will be the great wealth of which the Mormon church and its members privately are possessed. Then the oleaginous prophet will get a revelation to gird up his loins and to load the double-barrel shotgun, and fire the culverin, and to knock monogamy into a cocked hat. Money first and massacre second. They can draw on their revelation supply house at three days, any time, for authority to fill the irrigation ditches of Zion with the blood of the Gentile and feed his vital organs to the coyote.

(*Bill Nye's Remarks*, 1887)

Polygamy as a Religious Duty

During the past few years in the history of our republic, we have had leprosy, yellow fever and the dude, and it seemed as though each one would wreck the whole national fabric at one time. National and international troubles of one kind and another have gradually risen, been met and mastered, but the great national abscess known as the Church of Jesus Christ of Latter Day Saints still obstinately refuses to come to a head.

I may be a radical monogamist and a rash enthusiast upon this matter, but I still adhere to my original motto, one country, one flag and one wife at a time. Matrimony is a good thing, but it can be overdone. We can excuse the man who becomes a collector of rare coins, stamps, or autographs, but he who wears out his young life making a collection of wives, should be looked upon with suspicion.

After all, however, this matter has always been, and still is, treated with too much levity. It seems funny to us, at a distance of 1,600 miles, that a thick-necked patriarch in the valley of the Jordan should be sealed to thirteen or fourteen low-browed, half human females, and that the whole mass of humanity should live and multiply under one roof.

Those who see the wealthy polygamists of Salt Lake City do not know much of the horrors of trying to make polygamy and poverty harmonize in the rural districts. In the former case, each wife has a separate residence of suite or rooms, perhaps; but in the latter is the aggregation of vice and depravity doubly horrible because, instead of the secluded character which wickedness generally assumes, here it is the common heritage of the young and at once fails to shock or horrify.

Under the All-seeing eye, and the Bee Hive, and the motto, "Holiness to the Lord," with a bogus Bible and a red-nosed prophet who couldn't earn $13 per month pounding sand, this so-called church hanging on to the horns of the altar, as it were, defies the statutes, and while in open rebellion against the laws of God and man, refers to the constitution of the United States as protecting it in its "religious belief."

In a poem, the patient Mormon in the picturesque valley of the Great Salt Lake, where he has "made the desert blossom as the rose," looks well. With the wonderful music of the great organ at the tabernacle sounding in our ears, and the lofty temple nearby towering to the sky, you say to yourself, there is, after all, something solemn and impressive in all this; but when a greasy apostle in an alapaca duster takes his place behind the elevated desk, and with bad grammar and slangy sentences, asks God in a business-like way to bless this buzzing mass of unclean, low-browed, barbarous scum of all foreign countries, and the white trash and criminals of our own, you find no reverence, and no religious awe.

The same mercenary, heartless lunacy that runs through the sickly plagiarism of the Book of Mormon, pervades all this, and instead of the odor of sanctity you notice the flavor of bilge water, and the emigrant's own hailing sign, the all-pervading fragrance of the steerage.

Education is the foe of polygamy, and many of the young who have had the means by which to complete their education in the East, are apostate, at least so far as polygamy is concerned. Still, to the great mass of the poor and illiterate of Mormondom this is no benefit. The rich of the Mormon Church are rich because their influence with this great fraud has made them so; and it would, as a matter of business, injure their prospects to come out and bolt the nomination.

Utah, even with the Edmunds bill, is hopelessly Mormon; all adjoining States and Territories are already invaded by them, and the delegate in Congress from Wyoming is elected by the Mormon vote.

I believe that I am moderately liberal and free upon all religious matters, but when a man's confession of faith involves from three to twenty-seven old corsets in the back yard every spring, and a clothes line every Monday morning that looks like a bridal trousseau emporium struck by a cyclone, I must admit that I am a little bit inclined to be sectarian in my views.

It's bad enough to be slapped across the features by one pair of long wet hose on your way to the barn, but to have a whole bankrupt stock of cold, wet garments every week fold their damp arms around your neck, as you dodge under the clothes line to drive the cow out of the yard, is wrong.

It is not good for man to be alone, of course, but why should he yearn to fold a young ladies' seminary to his bosom? Why should this morbid sentiment prompt him to marry a Female Suffrage Mass Meeting? I do not wish to be considered an extremist in religious matters, but the doctrine that requires me to be sealed to a whole emigrant train, seems unnatural and inconsistent.

(*Bill Nye's Remarks*, 1887)

Spinal Meningitis

So many people have shown a pardonable curiosity about the above named disease, and so few have a very clear idea of the thrill of pleasure it affords the patient, unless they have enjoyed it themselves, that I have decided to briefly say something in answer to the innumerable inquiries I have received.

Up to the moment I had a notion of getting some meningitis, I have never employed a physician. Since then I have been thrown in their society a great deal. Most of them were very pleasant and scholarly gentlemen, who will not soon be forgotten; but one of them doctored me first for pneumonia, then for inflammatory rheumatism, and finally, when death was contiguous, advised me that I must have change of scene and rest.

I told him that if he kept on prescribing for me I thought I might depend on both. Change of physicians, however, saved my life. This horse doctor, a few weeks afterward, administered a subcutaneous morphine squirt in the arm of a healthy servant girl because she had the headache, and she is now with the rest of this veterinarian's patients in a land that is fairer than this.

She lived six hours after she was prescribed for. He gave her change of scene and rest. He has quite a thriving little cemetery filled with people who have succeeded in cording up enough of his change of scene and rest to last them through all eternity. He was called once to prescribe for a man whose head had been caved in by a stone match-box, and, after treating the man for asthma and blind staggers, he prescribed rest and change of scene for him too. The poor asthmatic is now breathing the extremely rarified air of the New Jerusalem.

Meningitis is derived from the Latin *Meninges*, membrane, and—*itis*, an affix denoting inflammation, so that, strictly speaking, meningitis is the inflammation of a membrane, and when applied to the spine, or cerebrum, is called spinal meningitis, or cerebrospinal meningitis, etc., according to the part of the spine or brain involved in the inflammation. Meningitis is a characteristic and result of so-called spotted fever, and by many it is deemed identical with it.

When we come to consider that the spinal cord, or marrow, runs down through the long, bony shaft made by the vertebrae, and that the brain and spine, though connected, are bound up in one continuous bony wall and covered with this inflamed membrane, it is not difficult to understand that the thing is very hard to get at. If your throat gets inflamed, a doctor asks you to run your tongue out into society about a yard and a half, and he pries your mouth open with one of Rogers Brothers' spoon handles. Then he is able to examine your throat as he would a page of the *Congressional Record*, and to treat it with some local application. When you have spinal meningitis, however, the doctor tackles you with bromides, ergots, ammonia, iodine, chloral hydrate, codi, bromide of ammonia, hasheesh, bismuth, valerianate of ammonia, morphine sulph., nux vomica, turpentine emulsion, vox humana, rex magnus, opium, cantharides, Dover's powders, and other bric-a-brac. These remedies are masticated and acted upon by the salivary glands, passed down the esophagus, thrown into the society of old gastric, submitted to the peculiar motion of the stomach and thoroughly chymified, then forwarded through the pyloric orifice into the smaller intestines, where they are touched up with bile, and later on handed over through the lacteals, thoracic duct, etc., to the vast circulatory system. Here it is yanked back and forth through the heart, lungs, and capillaries, and if anything is left to fork over to the disease, it has to squeeze into the long, bony, air-tight socket that holds the spinal cord. All this is done without seeing the patient's spinal cord before or after taking. If it could be taken out, and hung over a clothes line and cleansed with benzine, and then treated with insect powder, or rolled in corn meal, or preserved in alcohol, and then put back, it would be all right; but you can't. You pull a man's spine out of his system and he is bound to miss it, no matter how careful you have been about it. It is difficult to keep house without the spine. You need it every time you cook a meal. If the spinal cord could be pulled by a dentist and put away in pounded ice every time it gets a hot-box, spinal meningitis would lose its stinger.

I was treated by thirteen physicians, whose names I may give in a future article. They were, as I said, men I shall long remember. One of them said very sensibly that meningitis was generally over-doctored. I told him that I agreed with him. I said that if I should have another year of meningitis and thirteen more doctors, I would have to postpone my trip to Europe, where I had hoped to go and cultivate my voice. I've got a perfectly lovely voice if I could take it to Europe and have it sand-papered and varnished, and mellowed down with beer and bologna.

But I was speaking of my physicians. Sometime I am going to give their biographies and portraits, as they did those of Dr. Bliss, Dr. Barnes and others. Next year, if I can get railroad rates, I am going to hold a reunion of my physicians in Chicago. It will be a pleasant relaxation for them, and will save the lives of a large percentage of their patients.

(*Bill Nye's Remarks*, 1887)

CHAPTER 4

The Nation

The True American

The true American would rather work himself into luxury or the lunatic asylum than to hang like a great wart upon the face of nature.

(*Bill Nye's Chestnuts, Old and New*, 1887)

Accepting the Laramie Postoffice

Office of *Daily Boomerang*,
Laramie City, Wy., Aug. 9, 1882

My dear General.—I have received by telegraph the news of my nomination by the President and my confirmation by the Senate, as postmaster at Laramie, and wish to extend my thanks for the same.

I have ordered an entirely new set of boxes and postoffice outfit, including new corrugated cuspidors for the lady clerks.

I look upon the appointment, myself, as a great triumph of eternal truth over error and wrong. It is one of the epochs, I may say, in the Nation's onward march toward political purity and perfection. I do not know when I have noticed any stride in the affairs of state which so thoroughly impressed me with its wisdom.

Now that we are co-workers in the same department, I trust that you will not feel shy or backward in consulting me at any time relative to matters concerning postoffice affairs. Be perfectly frank with me and feel perfectly free to just bring anything of that kind right to me. Do not feel reluctant because I may at times appear haughty and indifferent, cold or reserved. Perhaps you do not think I know the difference between a general delivery window and a three-m quad, but that is a mistake.

My general information is far beyond my years.

With profoundest regard and a hearty endorsement of the policy of the President and the Senate, whatever it may be,

I remain, sincerely yours, BILL NYE, P. M.

Gen. Frank Hatton, Washington, D. C.

(*Bill Nye's Remarks*, 1887)

A Resign

POSTOFFICE DIVAN,
LARAMIE CITY, W. T., Oct. 1, 1883

To the President of the United States:

Sir.—I beg leave at this time to officially tender my resignation as postmaster at this place, and in due form to deliver the great seal and the key to the front door of the office. The safe combination is set on the numbers 33, 66 and 99, though I do not remember at this moment which comes first, or how many times you revolve the knob, or which direction you should turn it at first in order to make it operate.

There is some mining stock in my private drawer in the safe which I have not yet removed. This stock you may have if you desire it. It is a luxury but you may have it. I have decided to keep a horse instead of this mining stock. The horse may not be so pretty, but it will cost less to keep him.

You will find the postal cards that have not been used under the distributing table, and the coal down in the cellar. If the stove draws too hard, close the damper in the pipe and shut the general delivery window.

Looking over my stormy and eventful administration as postmaster here, I find abundant cause for thanksgiving. At the time I entered upon the duties of my office the department was not yet on a paying basis. It was not even self-sustaining. Since that time, with the active cooperation of the chief executive and the heads of the department I have been able to make our postal system a paying one, and on top of that I am now able to reduce the tariff on average-sized letters from three cents to two. I might add that this is rather too too, but I will not say anything that might seem undignified in an official resignation which is to become a matter of history.

Through all the vicissitudes of a tempestuous term of office I have safely passed. I am able to turn over the office today in a highly improved condition and to present a purified and renovated institution to my successor.

Acting under the advice of Gen. Hatton a year ago, I removed the feather bed with which my predecessor, Deacon Hayford, had bolstered up his administration by stuffing the window, and substituted glass. Finding nothing in the book of instructions, to postmasters which made the feather bed a part of my official duties, I filed it away in an obscure place and burned it in effigy, also in the gloaming. This act maddened my predecessor to such a degree that he then and there became a candidate for justice of the peace on the Democratic ticket. The Democratic party was able, however, with what aid it secured from the Republicans, to plow the old man under to a great degree.

It was not long after I had taken my official oath before an era of unexampled prosperity opened for the American people. The price of beef rose to a remarkable altitude, and other vegetables commanded a good figure and a ready market. We then began to make active preparations for the introduction of the strawberry-roan two-cent stamps and the black-and-tan postal note. One reform has crowded upon the heels of another until the country is today upon the foam-crested wave of permanent prosperity.

Mr. President, I cannot close this letter without thanking yourself and the heads of departments at Washington for your active, cheery and prompt cooperation in these matters. You can do as you see fit, of course, about incorporating this idea into your Thanksgiving proclamation, but rest assured it would not be ill-timed or inopportune. It is not alone a credit to myself. It reflects credit upon the administration also.

I need not say that I herewith transmit my resignation with great sorrow and genuine regret. We have toiled on together month after month, asking for no reward except the innate consciousness of rectitude and the salary as fixed by law. Now we are to separate. Here the roads seem to fork, as it were, and you and I, and the cabinet, must leave each other at this point.

You will find the key under the door-mat, and you had better turn the cat out at night when you close the office. If she does not go readily, you can make it clearer to her mind by throwing the cancelling stamp at her.

If Deacon Hayford does not pay up his box rent, you might as well put his mail in the general delivery, and when Bob Head gets drunk and insists on a letter from one of his wives every day in the week, you can salute him through the box delivery with an old Queen Anne tomahawk, which you will find near the Etruscan water pail. This will not in any manner surprise either of these parties.

Tears are unavailing. I once more become a private citizen, clothed only with the right to read such postal cards as may be addressed to me personally, and to curse the inefficiency of the postoffice department. I believe the voting class to be divided into two parties, viz: Those who are in the postal service, and those who are mad because they cannot receive a registered letter every fifteen minutes of each day, including Sunday.

Mr. President, as an official of this Government I now retire. My term of office would not expire until 1886. I must, therefore, beg pardon for my eccentricity in resigning. It will be best, perhaps, to keep the heart-breaking news from the ears of European powers until the dangers of a financial panic are fully past. Then hurl it broadcast with a sickening thud.

(*Bill Nye's Remarks*, 1887)

How the Glorious Fourth Was Celebrated at Whalen's Grove Last Year

There were patriotic remarks and greased-pig exercises at Whalen's Grove last year on the Fourth, all of which, according to the Sandy Mush *Record-Statesman*, passed off with marked success. From the opening prayer to the baseball contest and greased-pole doings, everything was harmonious, and the receipts were satisfactory. Col. L. Forsyth Heeley acted as marshal of the day, wearing a maroon sash, and mounted on his well-known horse, Mambrino King. A serious accident in the early morning was happily averted by Col. Heeley's coolness and self-possession. A lady from Lower Hominy, whose name could not be ascertained, while actively engaged in listening to the band, and holding her young child so that it could get a good view of the sun, became entangled in her train, which had worked around in front, and while recovering herself Col. L. Forsyth Heeley came down the street in advance of the fire laddies. The horse was rearing high in the air, and going sideways with a squeaking sound, which seemed to be caused by the friction between his second and third stomach. His mouth was wide open, and his fiery-red gums could be seen as far as the eye could reach. Almost every one thought there would be a holocaust; but at that trying instant, as if by magic, Col. Heeley decided to go down the other street.

Our fire laddies made a fine appearance, in their new, hot uniforms, and were not full during the parade, as was stated by the Hickory township *World*.

Everybody seemed to feel an interest in patriotism, with the exception of an old party from a distance, who opened the exercises by cutting a large watermelon and distributing it with a lavish hand among himself. He then went to sleep in the corner of a fence, where he would have been greatly pestered by flies if he had found out about it in time.

After a pleasant and courteous prayer by Rev. Mr. Meeks, in which he laid before the Lord a national policy which he felt certain would make a great hit, our Glee Club sang

Oh, say can you see,etc.

Judge Larraby read the Declaration of Independence in a rich dark red voice, and a self-made man from Hickory township delivered the following impromptu address, the manuscript of which he kindly furnished to the *Record-Statesman*:

"*Fellow Citizens*: This is the anniversary of the day when freedom towards all and malice towards none first got a foothold in this country. And we are now to celebrate that day. I say that on that day Tireny and uzurpation got a set-back that they will never recover from. We then paved the way for the poor, oppressed foreigner, so that he could come to our shores and take liberties with our form of government. To be a foreigner here in America today is one of the sweetest boons. If I could be just what I would like to be, I would be an oppressed foreigner, landing on our shores, free from the taxation and responsibility of government, with no social demands made on me, with nothing in my possession but a hearty Godspeed from both political parties, and a strong yearning for freedom. Oh, why was I not born an alien, that both parties wouldn't dast to reproach; an alien that can come here and find a government already established, with no flies on to it; a government of the people, by the people and for the people? (Fire-crackers and applause.)

"On the day that Button Gwinnett put his name to the statement that all men was created more or less equal, the spot on which we now stand was a howling wilderness. Where yonder lemonade-stand now stands and realizes a clean profit of forty-seven dollars and thirty-five cents on an investment of six dollars and fifty cents, the rank thistle nodded in the wynd, and the wild fox dag his hold unscared. If you do not believe this I refer you to the principal of our public school, who is today assisting in the band, and who is now in the act of up-ending his alto horn to pour out about a teacupful of liquid melody that he had left over from the last tune.

"And why is this? Why are we today a free people with a surplus in the treasury that nobody can get at? (Loud applause and squeal from a grass-fed horse tied to a tree who is being kicked by a red two-year-old, owned by the Pathmaster of Road District No. 3.)

"Why are our resources so great that they almost equal our liabilities? Why is everything done to make it pleasant for the rich man to accumulate more and more poverty? Why is it that so much is said about the tariff by men who do not support their families? Why is it that when we vote for a president of the United States, we have to take our choice between a statesmanlike candidate with great ability and proclivities for grand larceny—why is it that we are given our choice between this kind of a man and what Virgil refers to in his 'Childe Harold' as a chump? (Cheers and cries of 'That's so' from a man who is riveted to the spot by means of a new pitch-plank on which he is sitting and which will not permit him to move out of the sun.)

"One hundred years ago the tastes of our people were

simple. Now it takes so much simplicity to keep Congress going that the people don't get a chance at it. A century ago common, home-made rum was the only relaxation known to a plain but abstemious people. Now it takes a man with a mighty good memory to recall the names of some of the things he has drunk when his wife asks him about it on the following morning. I claim to have a good memory of names and things generally, but if you want to get me mixed up and have fun with me, you can do it that way.

"But, fellow-citizens, how can we best preserve the blessing of freedom and fork it over unimpaired to our children? How can we enchance the blood-bought right, which is inherent in every human being, of the people, for the people and by the people, where tyrant foot hath never trod nor bigot forged a chain, for to look back from our country's glorious natal day or forward to a glorious, a happy and a prosperous future with regard to purity of the ballot and free speech. I say for one we cannot do otherwise. (Prolonged applause.)

"I would rather have my right hand cleave to the roof of my mouth than to utter a sentiment that I would regret; but I say that as a people, as a nation or as an inalienable right which no man can gainsay or successfully controvert, not for political purposes, and yet I am often led to inquire whither are we drifting, not only as a people and as a nation, but as a country and as a joint school district, No. 6, where we now stand, and when we are paying a school teacher this summer twenty-two dollars a month to teach the children, little prattling children, during the hot summer weather, how many feet of intestines there are in the human body and what is best to do for it? Last winter we paid thirty-four dollars per month to a man who opened the school with prayer and then made a picture of the digestive organs on the blackboard. And still we wonder that politics is corrupt.

"I tell you that the seeds of vice and wickedness is often sowed at school in the minds of the young by teachers who are paid a large salary to do far different. What do you think of a man who would open a school with prayer and then converse freely about the alimentary canal? Such a man would lead a life of the deepest infamy if he had the least encouragement.

"So I say, fellow-citizens, that we must guard against the influences of the public schools as a nation, for the people, of the people, and by the people. Education is often a blessing in disguise, but we should not pry into things that the finite mind has no business with. How much was Galileo ahead in the long run for going out of his sphere? He was boycotted from morning till night and died poor. Look at Demosthenes. Look at Diogenes. They pried into science, and both of them was poor providers and have since died. Of course their names are frequently used in debating schools, and some claim that this is big pay for what they went through; but I say give me a high-stepping horse, the bright smile of dear ones who are not related to me in any way, the approval of the admiring throng, a large wooly dog that will do as I tell him, a modest little home and unlimited credit at the store, and I do not care how much B. will have to use off from the diameter of a given grindstone, for which he paid an undivided one-fifteenth.

"I know that this is regarded as a queer doctrine by what is called our more Advanced Thinkers, but I say let every man who pants for fame select his own style of pant and go ahead. I bid him a most hearty godspeed and hope he will do well.

"But what makes me mad is for a man to come to me and dictate what I shall pant for. This is called intolerance by people who can afford to use words of that size. Intolerance is a thing that makes me tired. Whether it's religious, political or social intolerance, I dislike it very much. People that think I will enjoy voting for a yaller dog that had been picked out for me, or that I will be tickled to death to indorse the religious dogmas of an effete monicky with my eyes shet, don't know me. I say, let every man rely solely on his own thinker, and damned be he who first cries hold, enough! I am not a profane man, but I quote from a poem in using the above quotation.

"But again. In closing, let me say that we owe it to our common country to be peaceable citizens and pay our taxes without murmuring. The time to get in our fine work is on the valuation, and it is too late to kick after that. Let us cultivate a spirit of lofty patriotism, but believe nothing just to oblige others. I used to be a great believer in anything that was submitted for my approval. That was what kept me back. Now, if a man like Jay Gould says he is not feeling so well as he did, I make him show me his tongue.

"We are here today to celebrate the birthday of American freedom, as I understand it, and I am here to say that whatever may be said against our refinement and our pork, our style of freedom is sought for everywhere. It is a freedom that will stand any climate and I hear it very highly spoken of wherever I go.

"I am here to state that, as boy and man, I have been a constant user of American freedom for over fifty years, and I can truly say that I feel no desire to turn back; also that there will be a grand, free-for-all scuffle for a greased pig on the vacant lot south of the church at seven o'clock, after which fireworks will be served to those who desire to remain."

And thus did the Fourth of July pass with all its glories in Whalen's Grove in the year of our independence the 110th.

(*Bill Nye's Chestnuts, Old and New*, 1887)

He Sees the Navy

It has become such a general practice to speak disrespectfully of the United States Navy that a few days ago I decided to visit the Brooklyn Navy Yard for the purpose of ascertaining, if possible, how much cause there might be for this light and airy manner of treating the navy, and, if necessary, to take immediate steps towards purifying the system.

I found that the matter had been grossly misrepresented, and that our navy, so far as I was able to discover, is self-sustaining. It has been thoroughly refitted and refurnished throughout, and is as pleasant a navy as one would see in a day's journey.

I had the pleasure of boarding the man-of-war Richmond under a flag of truce and the Atlantic under a suspension of the rules. I remained some time on board each of these war ships, and any man who speaks lightly of the United States Navy in my presence hereafter will receive a stinging rebuke.

The Brooklyn Navy Yard was inaugurated by the purchase of forty acres of ground in 1801. It has a pleasant water-front, which is at all times dotted here and there with new war vessels undergoing repairs. Since the original purchase others have been made and the land side of the yard inclosed by means of a large brick wall, so that in case there should be a local disturbance in Brooklyn the rioters could not break through and bite the navy. In this way a man on board the Atlanta while at anchor in Brooklyn is just as safe as he would be at home.

In order to enter and explore the Navy Yard it is necessary that one should have a pass. This is a safeguard, wisely adopted by the Commandant, in order to keep out strangers who might get in under the pretext of wishing to view the yard and afterwards attack one of the new vessels.

On the day I visited the Navy Yard just ahead of me a plain but dignified person in citizen's dress passed through the gate. He had the bearing of an officer, I thought, and kept his eye on some object about nine and one-fourth miles ahead as he walked past the guard. He was told to halt, but, of course, he did not do so. He was above it. Then the guard overhauled him, and even felt in his pockets for his pass, as I supposed. Concealed on his person the guard found four pint bottles filled with the essence of crime. They poured the poor man's rum on the grass and then fired him out, accompanied by a rebuke which will make him more deliberate about sitting down for a week or two.

The feeling against arduous spirits in the United States Navy is certainly on the increase, and the day is not far distant when alcohol in a free state will only be used in the arts, sciences, music, literature and the drama.

The Richmond is a large but buoyant vessel painted black. It has a front stairway hanging over the balcony, and the latch-string to the front door was hanging cheerily out as we drew alongside. During an engagement, however, on the approach of the enemy, the front stairs are hauled up and the latch-string is pulled in, while the commanding officer makes the statement, "April Fool," through a speaking-trumpet to the chagrined and infuriated foe.

The Richmond is a veteran of the late war, a war which no one ever regretted more than I did; not so much because of the bloodshed and desolation it caused at the time, but on account of the rude remarks since made to those who did not believe in the war and whose feelings have been repeatedly hurt by reference to it since the war closed.

The guns of the Richmond are muzzle-loaders, *i.e.*, the load or charge of ammunition is put into the other or outer end of the gun instead of the inner extremity or base of the gun, as is the case with the breech-loader. The breech-loader is a great improvement on the old style gun, making warfare a constant source of delirious joy now, whereas in former times in case of a naval combat during a severe storm, the man who went outside the ship to load the gun, while it was raining, frequently contracted pneumonia.

Modern guns are made with breeches, which may be easily removed during a fight and replaced when visitors come on board. A sort of grim humor pervades the above remark.

The Richmond is about to sail away to China. I do not

know why she is going to China but presume she does not care to be here during the amenities, antipathies and aspersions of a Presidential campaign. A man-of-war would rather make some sacrifices generally than to get into trouble.

I must here say that I would rather be captured by our naval officers than by any other naval officers I have ever seen. The older officers were calm and self-possessed during my visit on board both the Richmond and Atlanta, and the young fellows are as handsome as a steel engraving. While gazing on them as they proudly trod the quarter deck or any other deck that needed it, I was proud of my sex, and I could not help thinking that had I been an unprotected but beautiful girl, hostile to the United States, I could have picked out five or six young men there to either of whom I would be glad to talk over the details of an armistice. I could not help enjoying fully my hospitable treatment by the officers above referred to after having been only a little while before rudely repulsed and most cruelly snubbed by a haughty young cotton-sock broker in a New York store.

When will people ever learn that the way to have fun with me is to treat me for the time being as an equal?

It was wash-day on board ship, and I could not help noticing how the tyrant man asserts himself when he becomes sole boss of the household. The rule on board a man-of-war is that the first man who on wash-day shall suggest a "picked-up dinner" shall be loaded into the double-barrelled howitzer and shot into the bosom of Venus.

On the clothesline I noticed very few frills. The lingerie on board a war vessel is severe in outline and almost harsh in detail. Here the salt breezes search in vain for the singularly sawed-off and fluently trimmed toga of our home life. Here all is changed. From the basement to the top of the lightning rod, from pit to dome, as I was about to say, a belligerent ship on wash-day is not gayly caparisoned.

The Atlanta is a fair representative of the modern war vessel and would be the most effective craft in the world if she could use her guns. She has all the modern improvements, hot and cold water, electric lights, handy to depots and a good view of the ocean, but when she shoots off her guns they pull out her circles, abrade her deck, concuss her rotunda, confuse the main brace and injure people who have always been friendly to the Government. Her guns are now being removed and new circles put in, so that in future she would be enabled to give less pain to her friends and squirt more gloom into the ranks of the enemy. She is at present as useful for purposes of defense as a revolver in the bottom of a locked-up bureau drawer, the key of which is in the pocket of your wife's dress in a dark closet, wherein also the burglar is, for the nonce, concealed.

Politics has very little to do with the conduct of a navy-yard. No one would talk politics with me. I could not arouse any interest there at all in the election. Every one seemed delighted with the present Administration, however. The navy-yard always feels that way.

In the choky or brig at the guard-house I saw a sailor locked up who was extremely drunk.

"How did you get it here, my man?" I asked.

"Through thinflooonce of prominent Democrat, you damphool. Howje spose?" he unto me straightway did reply.

The sailor is sometimes infested with a style of arid humor which asserts itself in the most unlooked-for fashion. I laughed heartily at his odd yet coarse repartee, and went away.

The guard-house contains a choice collection of manacles, handcuffs, lily irons and other rare gems. The lily irons are not now in use. They consist of two iron bands for the wrist, connected by means of a flat iron, which can be opened up to let the wrists into place; then they are both locked at one time by means of a wrench like the one used by a piano-tuner. With a pair of lily irons on the wrists and another pair on the ankles a man locked in the brig and caught out 2,000 miles at sea in a big gale, with the rudder knocked off the ship and a large litter of kittens in the steam cylinder, would feel almost helpless.

I had almost forgotten to mention the drug store on board ship. Each man-of-war has a small pharmacy on the second floor. It is open all night, and prescriptions are carefully compounded. Pure drugs, paints, oils, varnishes and putty are to be had there at all times. The ship's dispensary is not a large room, but two ordinary men and a truss would not feel crowded there. The druggists treated me well on board both ships, and offered me my choice of antiseptics and anodynes, or anything else I might take a fancy to. I shall do my trading in that line hereafter on board ship.

The Atlanta has many very modern improvements, and is said to be a wonderful sailor. She also has a log. I saw it. It does not look exactly like what I had, as an old lumberman, imagined that it would.

It is a book, with writing in it, about the size of the tax-roll for 1888. In the cupola of the ship, where the wheel is located, there is also a big brass compass about as large as the third stomach of a cow. In this there is a little index or dingus, which always points towards the north. That is all it has to do. On each side of the compass is a large cannon ball so magnetized or polarized or influenced as to overcome the attraction of the needle for some desirable portion of the ship. There is also an index connected with the shaft whereby the man at the wheel can ascertain the position of the shaft and also ascertain at night whether the ship is advancing or retreating—a thing that he should inform himself about at the earliest possible moment.

The culinary arrangements on board these ships would make many a hotel blush, and I have paid $4 a day for a worse room than the choky at the guard-house.

In the Navy-Yard at Brooklyn is the big iron hull or running gears of an old ship of some kind which the Republicans were in the habit of hammering on for a few weeks prior to election every four years. Four years ago, through an oversight, the workmen were not called off nor informed of Blaine's defeat for several days after the election.

The Democrats have an entirely different hull in another part of the yard on which they are hammering.

The keel blocks of a new cruiser, 375 feet long, are just laid in the big ship-house at the Brooklyn Navy-Yard. She will be a very airy and cheerful boat, I judge, if the keel blocks are anything to go by.

In closing this account I desire to state that I hope I have avoided the inordinate use of marine terms, as I desire to make myself perfectly clear to the ordinary landsman, even at the expense of beauty and style of description. I would rather be thoroughly understood than confuse the reader while exerting myself to show my knowledge of terms. I also desire to express my thanks to the United States Navy for its kindness and consideration during my visit. I could have been easily blown into space half a dozen times without any opportunity to blow back through the papers, had the navy so desired, and yet nothing but terms of endearment passed between the navy and myself.

Lieut. Arthur P. Nazro, Chief Engineer Henry B. Nones, Passed Assistant Engineer E. A. Magee, Capt. F. H. Harrington, of the United States Marine Corps; Mr. Gus C. Roeder, Apothecary Henry Wimmer and the dog Zib, of the Richmond; Master Shipwright McGee, Capt. Miller, captain of the yard, and Mr. Milligan, apothecary of the Atlanta, deserve honorable mention for coolness and heroic endurance while I was there.

(*Bill Nye's Thinks*, 1888)

The Dubious Future

Without wishing to alarm the American people, or create a panic, I desire briefly and seriously to discuss the great question, "Whither are we drifting, and what is to be the condition of the coming man?" We cannot shut our eyes to the fact that mankind is passing through a great era of change; even womankind is not built as she was a few brief years ago. And is it not time, fellow citizens, that we pause to consider what is to be the future of the American?

Food itself has been the subject of change both in the matter of material and preparation. This must affect the consumer in such a way as to some day bring about great differences. Take, for instance, the oyster, one of our comparatively modern food and game fishes, and watch the effects of science upon him. At one time the oyster browsed around and ate what he could find in Neptune's back-yard, and we had to eat him as we found him. Now we take a herd of oysters off the trail, all run down, and feed them artificially till they swell up to a fancy size, and bring a fancy price. Where will this all lead at last, I ask as a careful scientist? Instead of eating apples, as Adam did, we work the fruit up into apple-jack and pie, while even the simple oyster is perverted, and instead of being allowed to fatten up in the fall on acorns and ancient mariners, spurious flesh is put on his bones by the artificial osmose and dialysis of our advanced civilization. How can you make an oyster stout or train him down by making him jerk a health lift so many hours every day, or cultivate his body at the expense of his mind, without ultimately not only impairing the future usefulness of the oyster himself, but at the same time affecting the future of the human race who feed upon him?

I only use the oyster as an illustration, and I do not wish to cause alarm, but I say that if we stimulate the oyster artificially and swell him up by scientific means, we not only do so at the expense of his better nature and keep him away from his family, but we are making our mark on the future race of men. Oyster-fattening is now, of course, in its infancy. Only a few years ago an effort was made at St. Louis to fatten cove oysters while in the can, but the system was not well understood, and those who had it in charge only succeeded in making the can itself more plump. But now oysters are kept on ground feed and given nothing to do for a few weeks, and even the older and overworked sway-backed and rickety oysters of the dim and murky past are made to fill out, and many of them have to put a gore in the waistband of their shells. I only speak of the oyster incidentally, as one of the objects toward which science has turned its attention, and I assert with the utmost confidence that the time will come, unless science should get a set-back, when the present hunting-case oyster will give place to the open-face oyster, grafted on the octopus and big enough to feed a hotel. Further than that, the oyster of the future will carry in a hip-pocket a flask of vinegar, half a dozen lemons and two little Japanese bottles, one of which will contain salt and the other pepper, and there will be some way provided by which you can tell which is which. But are we improving the oyster now? That is a question we may well ask ourselves. Is this a healthy fat which we are putting on him, or is it bloat? And what will be the result in the home-life of the oyster? We take him from all domestic influences whatever in order to make a swell of him by our modern methods, but do we improve his condition morally, and what is to be the great final result on man?

The reader will see by the questions I ask that I am a true scientist. Give me an overcoat pocket full of lower-case interrogation marks and a medical report to run to, and I can speak on the matter of science and advancement till Reason totters on her throne.

But food and oysters do not alone affect the great, pregnant future. Our race is being tampered with not only by means of adulterations, political combinations and climatic changes, but even our methods of relaxation are productive of peculiar physical conditions, malformations and some more things of the same kind.

Cigarette smoking produces a flabby and endogenous condition of the optic nerve, and constant listening at a telephone, always with the same ear, decreases the power of the other ear till it finally just stands around drawing its salary, but actually refusing to hear anything. Carrying an eight-pound cane makes a man lopsided, and the muscular and nervous strain that is necessary to retain a single eye-glass in place and keep it out of the soup, year after year, draws the mental stimulus that should go to the thinker itself, until at last the mind wanders away and forgets to come back, or becomes atrophied, and the great mental strain incident to the work of pounding sand or coming in when it rains is more than it is equal to.

Playing billiards, accompanied by the vicious habit of pounding on the floor with the butt of the cue ever and anon, produces at last optical illusions, phantasmagoria and visions of pink spiders with navy-blue abdomens. Baseball is not alone highly injurious to the umpire, but it also induces crooked fingers, bone spavin and hives among habitual players. Jumping the rope induces heart disease. Poker is unduly sedentary in its nature. Bicycling is highly injurious, especially to skittish horses. Boating induces malaria. Lawn tennis can not be played in the house. Archery is apt to be injurious to those who stand around and watch the game, and pugilism is a relaxation that jars heavily on some natures.

Football produces what may be called the endogenous or ingrowing toenail, stringhalt and mania. Copenhagen induces a melancholy, and the game of bean bag is unduly exciting. Horse racing is too brief and transitory as an out-door game, requiring weeks and months for preparation and lasting only long enough for a quick person to ejaculate "Scat!" The pitcher's arm is a new disease, the outgrowth of baseball; the lawn-tennis elbow is another result of a popular open-air amusement, and it begins to look as though the coming American would hear with one overgrown telephonic ear, while the other will be rudimentary only. He will have an abnormal baseball arm with a lawn-tennis elbow, a powerful football-kicking leg with the superior toe driven back into the palm of his foot. He will have a highly trained biceps muscle over his eye to retain his glass, and that eye will be trained to shoot a curved glance over a high hat and witness anything on the stage.

Other features grow abnormal, or shrink up from the lack of use, as a result of our customs. For instance, the man whose business it is to get along a crowded street with the utmost speed will have, finally, a hard, sharp horn growing on each elbow, and a pair of spurs growing out of each ankle. These will enable him to climb over a crowd and get there early. Constant exposure to these weapons on the part of the pedestrian will harden the walls of the thorax and abdomen until the coming man will be an impervious man. The citizen who avails himself of all modern methods of conveyance will ride from his door on the horse car to the elevated station, where an elevator will elevate him to the train and a revolving platform will swing him on board, or possibly the street car will be lifted from the surface track to the elevated track, and the passenger will retain his seat all the time. Then a man will simply hang out a red card, like an express card, at his door, and a combination car will call for him, take him to the nearest elevated station, elevate him, car and all, to the track, take him where he wants to go, and call for him at any hour of the night to bring him home. He will do his exercising at home, chiefly taking artificial sea baths, jerking a rowing machine or playing on a health lift till his eyes hang out on his cheeks, and he need not do any walking whatever. In that way the coming man will be over-developed above the legs, and his lower limbs will look like the desolate stems of a frozen geranium. Eccentricities of limb will be handed over like baldness from father to son among the dwellers in the cities, where every advantage in the way of rapid transit is to be had, until a metropolitan will be instantly picked out by his able digestion and rudimentary legs, just as we now detect the gentleman from the interior by his wild endeavors to overtake an elevated train.

In fact, Mr. Edison has now perfected, or announced that he is on the road to the perfection of, a machine which I may be pardoned for calling a storage think-tank. This will enable a brainy man to sit at home, and, with an electric motor and a perfected phonograph, he can think into a tin dipper or funnel, which will, by the aid of electricity and a new style of foil, record and preserve his ideas on a sheet of soft metal, so that when anyone says to him, "a penny for your thoughts," he can go to his valise and give him a piece of his mind. Thus the man who has such wild and beautiful thoughts in the night and never can hold on to them long enough to turn on the gas and get his writing materials, can set this thing by the head of his bed, and, when the poetic thought comes to him in the stilly night, he can think into a hopper, and the genius of Franklin and Edison together will enable him to fire it back at his friends in the morning while they eat their pancakes and glucose syrup from Vermont, or he can mail the sheet of tinfoil to absent friends, who may put it into their phonographs and utilize it. In this way the world may harness the gray matter of its best men, and it will be no uncommon thing to see a dozen brainy men tied up in a row in the back office of an intellectual syndicate, dropping pregnant thoughts into little electric coffee mills for a couple of hours a day, after which they can put on their coats, draw their pay, and go home.

All this will reduce the quantity of exercise, both mental and physical. Two men with good brains could do the thinking for 60,000,000 of people and feel perfectly fresh and rested the next day. Take four men, we will say, two to do the day thinking and two more to go on deck at night, and see how much time the rest of the world would have to go fishing. See how politics would become simplified. Conventions, primaries, bargains and sales, campaign bitterness and vituperation—all might be wiped out. A pair of political thinkers could furnish 100,000,000 of people with logical conclusions enough to last them through the campaign and put an unbiased opinion into a man's house each day for less than he now pays for gas. Just before election you could go into your private office, throw in a large dose of campaign whisky, light a campaign cigar, fasten your buttonhole to the wall by an elastic band, so that there would be a gentle pull on it, and turn the electricity on your mechanical thought supply. It would save time and money, and the result would be the same as it is now. This would only be the beginning, of course, and after a while every qualified voter who did not feel like exerting himself so much, need only give his name and proxy to the salaried thinker employed by the National Think Retort and Supply Works. We talk a great deal about the union of church and state, but that is not so dangerous, after all, as the mixture of politics and independent thought. Will the coming voter be an automatic, legless, hairless mollusk with an abnormal ear constantly glued to the tube of a big tank full of symmetrical ideas furnished by a national bureau of brains in the employ of the party in power?

(*A Guest at the Ludlow*, 1897)

Bill Nye Tells About New York's Custom House

It is reported that when Juan De Verazzano, in 1524, discovered the Bay of New York, and had been looked over from a therapeutic standpoint by Dr. Smith at Quarantine, he proceeded almost at once to select a site for a Custom House and place it in the hands of able men, several of whom are still at their desks in a pretty fair state of preservation.

The present Custom House is an imposing gray granite

architectural faux pas, with a low, retreating forehead like that of the pickerel. It is an inconvenient stone quarry with fluted columns, and, I would say, seems to be a cross between a long neglected cistern and a second hand sarcophagus.

If this be treason, make the most of it. I've already had an Indian outbreak this winter, and I do not mind a little set-to with the government, as I had funds left over after adjusting the Indian difficulty.

The New York Custom House is a triumph of inconvenience, a miracle of misfits and architectural deformities. It is a sort of compromise, so far as comfort goes, between the massive, rectangular residence of the cave dweller and the root cellar of the renaissance. There is no room in it, no elevator, no effort to be fireproof above the first floor, no light, no air, no method, no comfort and no economy. Venerable officials and employees who were there to show Henry Hudson over the building are still using the same tin cuspidors made of the inverted lid of the tin dinner pail of the past. The same sand is in them yet.

Monarchies have risen, flourished and decayed, kings have been born, cut their eye teeth, reigned a few lonesome weeks and moldered back into plebeian dust. Emperors have risen, and in a few years practically dictated to the world for a time, but their dust is in the mighty brickyard of the past, and the winds of heaven are whistling through the tattered upholstery of their vacant thrones, but the gray sand in the tin cuspidor of the Custom House of the United States smiles mockingly at the swift and hungry centuries.

The Custom House is ornamented with a big granite porch, supported by the government and a row of massive fluted columns as devoid of beauty as the animated drumstick of the antique chorus girl. This porch is expensive, but without use or beauty. In this respect it resembles the average case of typhoid imitative Englishman.

The first thing encountered in the interior is a rotunda, which presents the bright and ever changing scenery noticeable from the bottom of a drilled well. It started out to be the arena for a cockfight, changed its mind and sought to be a dry cistern; then securing a political pull it proceeded to become the rotunda of the Custom House, and every effort to remove it has so far proved unavailing.

Entering the large corner room where sits the collector of the port—and other dutiable beverages—I found Mr. Erhardt with his back to the fire and his face to the foe.

He comes down about nine a. m. and works till five o'clock in the evening, lunching in his office.

By hanging around till about one o'clock I was invited to lunch with him. Hon. James W. Husted sat and conversed while we ate. The artist will kindly make a rather pleasing drawing of the three scholarly gentlemen as they appeared at the time.

A man went by the door and looked cautiously in. Afterward I heard him say to another man that he understood the Sutherland Sisters were lunching together to-day. They then, both of them, burst into a low, coarse laugh.

The correspondence room is a very busy place, and hundreds of letters intended for the collector's private eyes are carefully opened and read by Mr. Jeffries, who came to New York in the fall of 1492, and at once went to work at his present job. I refer to this matter of correspondence because a great many people think that by marking a letter to a high official as private or personal it will be read only by him and immediately placed under his pillow at night. The collector can, however, have no secrets during office hours, at least through the mails, and hardly viva voce.

The cashier's room interested me a good deal. It always does wherever I go. So, with the collector to vouch for me, I went through two little dingy offices and dens where as high as a million and a half per day is handled. This money, as Colonel Jones explained, is either in the form of a specially certified check or currency, and the latter is constantly assorted into the proper denominations, so that at the time for handing over to the sub-treasury at evening, quarters are in their proper parcels, duly counted, so likewise small change and large up to the ten thousand dollar bill which I held in my hand quite a while, meantime asking Colonel Jones to notice what a peculiarly mottled appearance the sky had.

However, with a suspicion growing, I dare say, out of his long and busy contact with sharpers and men of little principle, he watched me eagerly, I noticed, and sent an employee to the window to look at the peculiarly mottled appearance of the sky.

One of the best experts on bills and silver counterfeits in the country, no doubt, has his little cage in the cashier's office. He cannot always explain why he does not like a bill or a silver piece, but he knows he does not choose any of it, and a test shows that he is correct. Long after I had left this department Colonel Jones showed me a $20 bill, and asked me if I saw anything peculiar about it. I said no, I did not, aside from the fact that a $20 bill always did have a novel appearance to me.

"Well," said he, "that is a counterfeit. It was detected just after you went out."

I convinced him after a while that I did not do it, though.

The bill had been dimly photographed, and then all the work, back and front, carefully done over with a pen. It was a pretty good looking bill. Mr. Urban detected it while a nervous person would be engaged in ejaculating the words Jack Robinson. Mr. Urban is one of the men who holds his office by right of eternal fitness, and nobody ever ventures to ask him what his politics may be or used to be. It is a secret between him and high heaven. This is the way it should be.

If a man could make himself absolutely necessary to his employer or his government, and then remain there at his post instead of having to go out for three months every year to yell for his party till the rich, ripe rum mantled to his luscious bugle, there would be a net saving to the world in two hundred years that would buy some man a nice little farm.

The cashier's office has a system of three checks, whereby the counter, the bookkeeper and the teller are guarding against each other's mistakes, and so accurate is this matter that in a day's work ranging from $400,000 to $1,500,000 the footings of the three are alike to a cent.

The certified check, in the ordinary sense of the term, does not go at the Custom House. The bank may be ever so good; its certificate must be to the effect that so much money is on deposit to its credit at the sub-treasury, and when that account is overdrawn, if only for five cents, that check waits till the account is made good again.

When you pay duties the fact that you are the president of a bank or the head of a family does not count. Ready money or the certificate of the sub-treasury alone goes.

In one corner of the cashier's department is a headsman's block, near it a stellated punch and a sledge hammer. When a coin is found to be worthless it is carefully laid on this block, the pinking iron is placed upon it and then a strong man hits it a welt with the sledge.

After knocking the essential tar out of the coin, as one may say, it is politely returned to the owner, who has to make it good. The idea, as the bright eyed reader has already discovered, no doubt, is to prevent its circulation, and that is almost invariably the result.

Civil service has its odd and rather amusing features to one, at least, who sees the ridiculous readily. For instance, there is a position under the government in the customs which requires that a man who fills it shall, to the best of his ability, knock off the lids of boxes by means of a cold chisel and hammer.

The knowledge of Euclid or the binormal theorem is not absolutely necessary, the principal thing being to avoid pulling out the thumb nail while pulling the other nails. But the civil service requires that he shall know certain things, whether he can knock off the lid of a box or not. One of these men has to stand upon a set of cyclopedias in order to reach the top of a big box.

In the language of a friend, "he is up on books, but he is

short on stature." The civil service does not ask him how tall he is, but whether a given line, bisecting the base of an isosceles triangle and running due east toward a given point, will also bisect the circumference of a given circle whose radius is perpendicular to the base of the isosceles triangle.

Take also the case of a man whose duty it is to pack and unpack valuable bric-a-brac. Those who have put in a year or two packing and unpacking without breakage costly china, marble, glass and other truck will agree with me that this is extremely important, although a civil service examination does not touch the question. Of course, it is well for a man who drives a team for the Custom House to know that "evolution is a gradual change from an infinite, incoherent homogeneity to a definite, coherent heterogeneity through continuous differentiations and integrations," but it would be still better if he knew promptly what to do in a malignant case of botts.

But I cannot do this subject justice, and perhaps I should not refer to it here, because it really does not belong to a letter treating of the Custom House, for the cases above referred to were obtained surreptitiously from other parties. The collector seemed to take kindly to civil service, I judged, and although he courteously laughed when I referred to these illustrations, he did not give way to mirth as I have seen people do.

He is kind to those who have served well and faithfully, and seems to cling to faithful employees wherever the public weal requires it or will be best subserved. I think that is what he said, though the word weal is one that I know very little of. He says that gross incompetence, intemperance or indolence would always meet with a prompt dismissal.

"And what would you regard as a pronounced case of indolence in the service of the government, Mr. Erhardt?"

"Well, the government is not generally severe on its employees, I think. For instance, I knew of a man who acted for many years as a watchman for the government, and while the President was down there at Washington this man held up this corner of the great national fabric by attending the theatre while on watch. He slept at the government building, but took his meals at home. Thus he got his salary for his lodging, and often received a box at the theatre on the strength of his relations with the government. He is now not in it."

"But regarding long continued attacks of indolence, does the government fire such cases?"

"Yes, always. Ultimately. The policy of the government has been rather pacific, and yet where a man has become so sedentary that he can sit down on an open Barlow knife and go to sleep we look into his case. Should he occupy all day a chair on which there is an open eight-bladed knife, with a corkscrew in the back, also open, and then at night go home with the knife adhering to his person, we call for his resignation."

Speaking about chairs, while I was in the office word came that there had been orders issued from Washington that some of the office furniture should be repaired. It seems that some time ago a special agent of that department called on the collector. The latter showed him a chair. The agent said he did not care to sit. "Yes, yes, sit down," said the genial cherub who presides over the revenue and sits serene beneath the peculiar banner of the Custom House; "take that chair right there."

The agent did so, and the collector conversed with him. Every little while the agent would put some more chalk on the leather seat of the chair and remount it, but in a few minutes he would fall off, and just barely catch himself and get out of the way before the chair stumbled and fell on him. Finally he said he guessed he must go, and as he did so the revolutionary chair slid out from under him, and, going over in the corner, crossed its legs and put its arms behind its back.

"Now," said the collector, "I beg your pardon for offering you that chair, but I wanted to ask you if it would be possible to get hold of an appropriation from which a suitable amount could be secured for the purpose of fixing that chair. There isn't a bareback rider in the United States who can keep his seat there over two and one-half minutes at present, and I am tired of replacing people who have fallen off that chair."

It is going to be repaired now. Also a man who cleans cisterns is going to whitewash the rotunda if the government would not deem it a mare's nest.

I sometimes think that if the United States would give more time to large affairs, like reciprocity and statesmanship, instead of running wildly a mile and a half every time an old mare flies cackling joyously from the nest, we would have more groceries in the house for a given sum than we now have.

(*The Funny Fellows Grab-Bag*, 1903)

CHAPTER 5

The Muses and Their Kin

The Muse

Criticism on the Works of the Sweet Singer of Michigan

Through the courtesy of a popular young lady of Chicago, who recognizes struggling genius at all times I have been permitted to carefully read and enjoy the lays of the sweet singer of Michigan; and I ask the reader to come with me a few moments into the great field of literature, while we flit from flower to flower on the wings of the Muse.

There are few, indeed, of us who do not love the heaven-born music of true poesy. Hardened, indeed, must be he whose soul is dead to the glad song of the true poet, and we can but pity the gross, brutal nature which refuses to throb and burn with spiritual fire lighted with coals from the altar of the gods.

I speak only for myself when I say that seven or eight twangs of the lyre stir my impressible nature so that I rise above the cares and woes of this earthly life, and I paw the ground and yearn for the unyearnable, and howl.

Julia A. Moore,* better known as the Sweet Singer of Michigan, was born some time previous to the opening of

*See "Answers to Correspondents," *infra*, for an additional segment relating to Julia A. Moore.—Ed.

this chapter, of poor but honest parents, and although she couldn't have custard pie and frosted cake every day she was middling chipper, as appears by a little poem in the collection entitled "The Author's Early Life," in which she says:

> My heart was gay and happy;
> This was ever in my mind,
> There is better days a coming,
> And I hope some day to find
> Myself capable of composing.
> It was my heart's delight
> To compose on a sentimental subject
> If it came in my mind just right.

This would show that the Muse was getting in its work, as I might say, even while yet Julia was a little nut-brown maid trudging along to school with bare feet that looked like the back of a warty toad. In my visions I see her now standing in front of the teacher's desk, soaking the first three joints of her thumb in her rosebud mouth, and trying to work her off toe into a knot-hole in the floor, while outside, the turtle-dove and the masculine Michigan mule softly coo to their mates.

A portrait of the author appears on the cover of the little volume. It is a very striking face. There are lines of care about the mouth—that is, part way around the mouth. They did not reach all the way around because they didn't have time. Lines of care are willing to do anything that is reasonable, but they can't reach around the North Park without getting fatigued. These lines of care and pain look to the student of physiognomy as though the author had lost a good deal of sleep trying to compose obituary poems. The brow is slightly drawn, too, as though her corns might be hurting her. Julia wears her hair plain, like Alfred Tennyson and Sitting Bull. It hangs down her back in perfect abandon and wild profusion, shedding bear's oil over the collar of her delaine dress, regardless of expense.

I can not illustrate or describe the early vision of dimpled loveliness which Julia presented in her childhood, better than by giving a little gem from "My Infant Days":

> When I was a little infant
> And I lay in mother's arms,
> Then I felt the gentle pressure
> Of a loving mother's arms.
>
> "Go to sleep my little baby,
> Go to sleep," mamma would say;
> "O, will not my little baby
> Go to sleep for ma today?"

When I read this little thing the other day it broke me all up. It took me back to my childhood days when I lay in my little trundle bed, and was wakeful, and had a raging thirst, insomuch that I used to want a drink of water every fifteen seconds. Mamma didn't ask if I would "go to sleep for ma, today." She used to turn the bed-clothes back over the footboard, so that she could have plenty of sea room, and then she would take an old sewing-machine belt, and it would sigh through the agitated air for a few moments pretty plenty, till the writer of these lines would conclude to sob himself to sleep, and anon through the night he would dream that he had backed up against the Hill Smelting Works. That's the kind of "Go to sleep for ma today" that comes up vividly to my mind.

But I must give another stanza or two from Julia's collection as showing how this gifted writer can with a word dispel the chilling temperature of December, and run the thermometer up to 100 degrees in the shade. I will quote from the death of "Little Henry":

> It was on the eleventh of December,
> On a cold and windy day,
> Just at the close of evening,
> When the sunlight fades away,
> Little Henry he was dying,
> In his little crib he lay,
> With the soft winds around him sighing,
> From early morn till close of day.

One of Julia's poems opens out in such a cheerful, pleasant way that I wish I could give it all, but space forbids. She tunes her lyre so that it will mash all right, and then says:

Come all kind friends, both far and near,
O, come, and see what you can hear.

Then she proceeds to slaughter some one. In looking over her poems one is struck with the terrible mortality which they show. Julia is worse than a Gatling gun. I have counted twenty-one killed and nine wounded, in the small volume which she has given to the public. In giving the circumstances which attended the death of one of her subjects, and the economical principles of the deceased, she says:

And he was sick and very bad,
Poor boy, he thought, no doubt
If he came home in a smoking car
His money would hold out.
He started to come back alone,
He came one-third the way.
One evening, in the car alone,
His spirit fled away.

That's the way Julia kills off a young man just as we get interested in him. You just begin to like one of her heroes or heroines and Julia proceeds to lay said hero or heroine out colder than a wedge. A sad, sad thing, which goes to the tune of Belle Mahone, starts out as follows:

"Once there lived a lady fair,
With black eyes and curly hair;
She has left this world of care,
Sweet Carrie Monroe."

To which I have added in my poor weak way—

She could not her sorrows bear,
For she was a dumpling rare;
She has clum the golden stair,
Sweet Carrie Monroe.

'Twas indeed a day of gloom
When we gathered in her room,
While she cantered up the flume,
Sweet Carrie Monroe.

I will give but one more example of Julia's exquisite word painting, and then after a word or two relative to her style generally I will close.

After speaking tearfully of her life as a child, she says:

My childhood days have passed and gone,
And it fills my heart with pain,
To think that youth will never more
Return to me again.
And now, kind friends, what I have wrote
I hope you will pass o'er,
And not criticize, as some have done,
Hitherto herebefore.

I know that it ill becomes me to assume the prerogative of criticizing a poet's style or even to suggest any improvements, but sometimes an outsider may be able to stand off as it were and see little defects in a masterpiece which the author can not see.

My idea would be to take these poems and remove the crown sheet, then put in a new running gear, upset and bush the pitman, kalsomine the boiler plate, drill new holes in the eccentric, rim out the gas pipe, raise the posterior eccentric to a level with the gang plank, slide the ash pan forward of the monkey wrench, securing it by draw bars to the top-gallant mizzen. Then, throwing open the condenser and allowing the cerebellum to rest firmly against the vicarious whippety-whop, fair time may be made on a gentle grade.

If I were to suggest anything further it would be that Julia have entire change of air and surroundings. Michigan is too healthy for an ambitious obituary poet. She naturally has too much time on her hands. Let her go into the yellow fever districts next summer, where she can work in two or three of her cheerful little funeral odes every morning before breakfast. That's the place for her. It may kill her, but if it should we will trust in Providence to raise up some inspired idiot to take her place. We will struggle along anyway with George Francis Train and Denis Kearney and Dr. Mary Walker, even if Julia joins the glad throng of poets who let their hair grow long and kick up their heels in the green fields of Eden.

One more suggestion which will, I know, be accepted as coming from one who never says anything but in the kindest spirit. I think that Julia takes advantage of her poetic license. A poetic license, as I understand it, simply allows the poet to jump the 15 over the 14 in order to bring in the proper rhyme, but it does not allow the writer to usurp the management of the entire system of worlds, and introduce dog-days and ice cream between Christmas and New Year. It does not in any way allow the contractor of prize funeral puffs to sandwich a tropical evening with the scent of orange blossom and mignonette, in between two December days in Michigan, that would freeze the lightning rods off the houses, and when the owners of cast iron dogs have to bring them in, and stand them behind the parlor stove.

Julia can't fool me much on a Michigan winter. When the seductive breath from the north comes soughing across Lake Superior, redolent with the blossom rock of the copper mines, and dead cranberry vines, and slippery elm bark, the poet or poetess who could maliciously crawl into a buffalo overcoat, and write a dirge that worked in "sighing soft winds," just for the benefit of one whose spirit is in a land where house plants never freeze, should have no poetic license. I would be in favor of having such license revoked, or raising the price so high that none but good, reliable, square-toed poets could practice. I would suggest $500 per year for poets driving one horse, and dealing in native poems on death, spring, beautiful snow, etc., etc.; $1,000 per year for two horse, platform spring poets, retailers of imported poems; and $1,500 per year for poets who do a general business in manufactured Havana poems, or native wrappers with Havana fillers.

We have too many poets in our glorious republic who ought to be peeling the epidermis off a bull train; and too many poetesses who would succeed better boiling soap-grease, or spiking a 6 × 8 patch on the quarter-deck of a faithful husband's overalls.

I do not refer entirely to Julia in the last few lines, for Julia is not deserving of such criticism. She was never intended to do the drudgery of housework. She is too frail. She couldn't cook, because her cake would be sad, and her soft, wavy hair, like the mane of a Cayuse plug, would get in the codfish balls, and cling to the butter.

No, Julia, you don't look like a woman whose career as a housewife would be a success. From the mournful look in your limpid eye, I would say that your lignum-vitae bread, and celluloid custard pie, and indestructible waffles, and fireproof pancakes, and burglar-proof chicken pie, would give you away. Your mind would be far away in the poet's realm, and you would put shoe blacking in the blanc mange, and silver gloss starch in the tea, and cod liver oil in the sponge cake. So, Julia, you may continue right along as you are doing. It don't do much harm, and no doubt it does you a heap of good.

(*Bill Nye and Boomerang*, 1881)

Bankrupt Sale of Literary Gems

Office of the Mormon Bazoo

Little boys who are required by their teacher to write compositions at school can save a great deal of unnecessary worry and anxiety by calling on the editor of this paper, and glancing over the holiday stock of second-hand poems and essays. Debating clubs and juvenile lyceums supplied at a large reduction. The following are a few selections, with price:

"Old Age," a poem written in red ink, price ten cents. "The Dog," blank verse, written on foolscap with a hard pencil, five cents. "Who will love me all the while?" a tale, price three cents per pound. "Hold me in your clean white arms," song and dance, by the author of "Beautiful Snow," price very reasonable; it must be sold. "She ain't no longer mine, nor I ain't hern," or the sad story of two sundered hearts; spruce gum and licorice taken in exchange for this piece. "God: his attributes and peculiarities," will be sold at a cent and a half per pound, or traded for a tin dipper for the office. Give us a call before purchasing elsewhere.

The stock on hand must be disposed of in order to give place to the new stock of odes and sonnets on Spring and contributions on "the violet" and the "skipful lamb."

(*Bill Nye and Boomerang*, 1881)

Fiction

One of the very noticeable improvements of the age in the literary line is the remarkable bracing up of the mental faculties of those who write fiction. From the Sabbath school book to the more elaborate novel, there has been in the past few years a pronounced effort on the part of those who erect this class of literature to introduce so far as possible characters who resemble live people.

Not many years ago the boss heroine of the prevailing novel could not catch the popular eye without being so artistically scrumptuous that she could walk over a bed of violets and not scrunch a single one. Now it is not unusual to ring in a leading lady who weighs 125 pounds, and who can eat a dozen fried oysters at the expense of the hero of the story. We can remember back to the time when, according to the average novel, a young lady could cross the plains in a Swiss muslin dress with short sleeves, and with satin slippers and silk clocked hose.

It was not an uncommon occurrence for a frail girl who had been the pampered child of luxury all her life to be kidnapped by hostile Indians about four miles from Chicago and carried away into the wigwam of the red man in a ball dress.

The all-wool facts in the case generally show that when a Caucasian woman from Chicago is captured by the Indians, she has to sit astride on a lame bronco and ride all day clothed in the uniform of a private soldier.

Pictures of beautiful white girls sitting on the back of an ambling palfrey and looking like Rowena riding to the castle of Front de Beuf, will hardly go down. Captive maidens in the hands of the Indians are in luck if they can ride at all. A picture representing the pale prairie flower walking over the velvety cactus in her stocking feet, and holding on to the tail of the chief's pony, would be more life-like, although it might mar the stage effect of the book.

In later years, however, people are introduced into books who wear overcoats and ulsterettes when it is cold, and who eat, and get vaccinated, and quarrel, and lie abed in the morning, and act like the balance of mankind.

Stories about languid young gentlemen who do not have to work, and who, although showing up no visible means of support, don't seem to feel called upon to do anything but stroll at set of sun or stretch themselves at the foot of some venerable oak and let the 1,000-legged worms crawl up their trowsers legs, are apparently losing their grip.

Formerly it was not the thing for a young man in a book to get mad. If he did so it was in such an unnatural style, and his remarks sounded so much like reading from manuscript, that the reader couldn't help pitying him. The high-salaried hero of those days either allowed the leading villain to get up and walk over him and grind him into the sod without resenting it, or he got on his ear at nothing and made a post mortem examination of the villain with a Spanish hay knife because he said the heroine had a freckle on her nose.

Another noticeable and highly praiseworthy change is the falling off in the horrible mortality in recent fiction. It was not an uncommon thing at one time in the history of literary prevarication for a brave young Apollo, bearded like a buffalo robe, to roll up his pants legs about four feet and wade through a torrent of gore every Monday and Wednesday evening, with sanguinary matinee on Saturday afternoons.

Now the style is changing. When the author wants to introduce some carnage he don't butcher a tribe of Sioux and spread their busted remains all over Dakota in fifteen minutes. He just throws in a railroad collision or the burning of a theater and lets it go at that.

The plot of modern stories is a little more human than it used to be and a little more diversified. Nowadays you can't tell for an absolute certainty whether Reginald will marry the girl in the thirty-first chapter or not. He may be dead or divorced from another woman before he gets to the third chapter.

You cannot gamble on it any more. Modern fiction has reached that pass where the twentieth chapter may wind up with a funeral of twins. Death or dyspepsia may befall the hero at any moment, and the old-time schedule has been abandoned. It is as delightfully surprising as prospecting for a quartz lead. You may discover a bonanza or sit down on a tarantula at any moment. You may tumble out of an ore bucket and reach the foot of the shaft with your shoulder blade in your pistol pocket, or you may sit down on an ostensibly extinct blast to think over your past life and the next moment go crashing through the milky way without clothes enough to keep off the night air.

(*Forty Liars, and Other Lies*, 1882)

Uncle Tom's Cabin

Thursday evening the novel and startling drama of Uncle Tom's Cabin was rendered here by the Anthony & Ellis company.

As the play is a comparatively new one, there being only forty or fifty Uncle Tom combinations now on the road, some traveling in special cars and others by handcar and special tie rates, we give a kind of synopsis of the drama.

Mr. George Harris is supposed to be a calcimined mulatto, who is perplexed with doubts about who his parents were, on his father's side, and Eliza, his wife, is situated in a similar manner. Their little boy is the only member of the family who has a pedigree that will bear investigation at all.

Mr. Harris and wife are endeavoring throughout the play to get to Canada, where they intend to go into the restaurant business and acquire scads.

Mrs. Harris, in making her escape across the river, which is filled with large chunks of cordwood painted light blue, is followed by two blood hounds with iron cake baskets over their heads, and two men with false beards made out of buffalo robes.

Uncle Tom's Cabin is an extremely fatal play, there being four killed and three wounded in three hours. Little Eva is the first to succumb to the extremely malarious and unhealthy climate. After that her father expires on a $2 bedstead, with a sheet thrown over him and his boots on. They all die easy, to pianissimo music. Thursday evening, as Eva was dying, and her little breath came thick and fast, the janitor went around and filled up the coal stoves to hide his emotion, and two gentlemen on the south side of the opera house were so carried away with conflicting emotions that they sought consolation in a four-quart job lot of peanuts and hoarhound candy.

The next untimely death is that of Uncle Tom, who is

supposed to get whelted over the head with the butt end of a loaded whip. This, however, is an optical illusion, because we asked Mr. Legree on the following day if he got a fresh Uncle Tom at each and every performance, or how he fixed it, and he said that he wouldn't try to conceal anything from us, but just tell us plainly how it was.

It seems that he does not kill Uncle Tom at all. He said he had nothing in particular against the old man, so he just backed him up against the scenery and hit a glancing lick that was more fatal to the scenery than it was to Uncle Tom. He said that Tom stood in with him, and when the proper moment arrived for the sickening thud, generally clapped his hands together to heighten the effect.

After awhile Mr. Legree is killed also. He is massacred with a large bread knife and is dragged off the stage by a hired man.

The donkey generally brought in by Lawyer Marks sometimes introduces a melodrama that is not down in the bills. Once, while showing in Utah, one of the university students, who sings falsetto, got mad at the donkey because the animal was attracting more attention and drawing a larger salary than he was, and so just before the donkey was to go on, and while he was waiting for his cue, the university student poured about a gill of turpentine into the ear of the timid little public favorite.

When he got in where the auction sale was going on, the meek little animal seemed excited about something. He scattered Mr. Marks around among the footlights and knocked Mr. Legree through the bass viol. Most of the actors excused themselves and retired. Then the household pet got over into the orchestra and went through with some calisthenics. Also through some of the musicians.

For awhile it looked as though not only the entire troupe but the orchestra and most of the audience would go up the golden stair with Little Eva.

"Uncle Tom's Cabin" has been on the stage twenty years now, but it is about as reliable as a promoter of the scalding tear as ever it was. It is a play that takes first rate in this dry climate and saves the expense of irrigation, to a great extent.

(*Forty Liars, and Other Lies*, 1882)

Julius Caesar in Town

The play of "Julius Caesar," which has been at the Academy of Music this week, has made a great hit. Messrs. Booth and Barrett very wisely decided that if it succeeded here it would do well anywhere. If the people of New York like a play and say so, it is almost sure to go elsewhere. Judging by this test the play of "Julius Caesar" has a glowing future ahead of it. It was written by Gentlemen Shakespeare, Bacon and Donnelly, who collaborated together on it. Shakespeare did the lines and plot, Bacon furnished the cipher and Donnelly called attention to it through the papers.

The scene of "Julius Caesar" is laid in Rome just before the railroad was completed to that place. In order to understand the play itself we must glance briefly at the leading characters which are introduced and upon whom its success largely depends.

Julius Caesar first attracted attention through the Roman papers by calling the attention of the medical faculty to the now justly celebrated Caesarian operation. Taking advantage of the advertisement thus attained, he soon rose to prominence and flourished considerably from 100 to 44 B.C., when a committee of representative citizens and property-owners of Rome called upon him and on behalf of the people begged leave to assassinate him as a mark of esteem. He was stabbed twenty-three times between Pompey's Pillar and eleven o'clock, many of which were mortal. This account of the assassination is taken from a local paper and is graphic, succinct and lacks the sensational elements so common and so lamentable in our own time. Caesar was the implacable foe of the aristocracy and refused to wear a plug hat up to the day of his death. Sulla once said, before Caesar had made much of a showing, that some day this young man would be the ruin of the aristocracy, and twenty years afterwards when Caesar sacked, assassinated and holocausted a whole theological seminary for saying "eyether" and "nyether," the old settlers recalled what Sulla had said.

Caesar continued to eat pie with a knife and in many other ways to endear himself to the masses until 68 B.C., when he ran for Quaestor. Afterward he was Aedile, during the term of which office he sought to introduce a number of new games and to extend the limit on some of the older ones. From this to the Senate was but a step. In the Senate he was known as a good Speaker, but ambitious, and liable to turn up during a close vote when his enemies thought he was at home doing his chores. This made him at times odious to those who opposed him, and when he defended Cataline and offered to go on his bond, Caesar came near being condemned to death himself.

In 62 B.C. he went to Spain as Propraetor, intending to write a book about the Spanish people and their customs as soon as he got back, but he was so busy on his return that he did not have time to do so.

Caesar was a powerful man with the people, and while in the Senate worked hard for his constituents, while other Senators were having their photographs taken. He went into the army when the war broke out, and after killing a great many people against whom he certainly could not have had anything personal, he returned, headed by the Rome Silver Cornet Band and leading a procession over two miles in length. It was at this time that he was tendered a crown just as he was passing the City Hall, but thrice he refused it. After each refusal the people applauded and encored him till he had to refuse it again. It is at about this time the play opens. Caesar had just arrived on a speckled courser and dismounted outside the town. He comes in at the head of the procession with the understanding that the crown is to be offered him just as he crosses over to the Court-House.

Here Cassius and Brutus meet, and Cassius tries to make a Mugwump of Brutus, so that they can organize a new movement. Mr. Edwin Booth takes the character of Brutus and Mr. Lawrence Barrett takes that of Cassius. I would not want to take the character of Cassius myself, even if I had run short of character and needed some very much indeed, but Mr. Barrett takes it and does it first-rate. Mr. Booth also plays Brutus so that old settlers here say it seems almost like having Brutus here among us again.

Brutus was a Roman republican with strong tariff tendencies. He was a good extemporaneous after-dinner speaker and a warm personal friend of Caesar, though differing from him politically. In assassinating Caesar, Brutus used to say afterwards he did not feel the slightest personal animosity, but did it entirely for the good of the party. That is one thing I like about politics—you can cut out a man's vitals and hang them on the Christmas tree and drag the fair name of his wife and mother around through the sewers for six weeks before election, and so long as it is done for the good of the party it is all right.

So when Brutus is authorized by the caucus to assassinate Caesar he feels that, like being President of the United States, it is a disagreeable job; but if the good of the party seems really to demand it he will do it, though he wishes it distinctly understood that personally he hasn't got a thing against Caesar.

In act 4 Brutus sits up late reading a story by E. P. Roe, and just as he is in the most exciting part of it the ghost of the assassinated Caesar appears and states that it will meet him with hard gloves at Philippi. Brutus looked bored and says that he is not in condition, but the ghost leaves it that way and Brutus looks still more bored till the ghost goes out through a white oak door without opening it.

At Philippi, Brutus sees that there is no hope of police interference, and so before time is called he inserts his sword into his being and dies while the polite American audience puts on its overcoat and goes out, looking over its shoulder to see that Brutus does not take advantage of this moment, while the people are going away, to resuscitate himself.

The play is thoroughly enjoyable all the way through, especially Caesar's funeral. The idea of introducing a funeral and engaging Mark Antony to deliver the eulogy, with the understanding that he was to have his traveling expenses paid and the privilege of selling the sermon to a syndicate, shows genius on the part of the joint authors. All the way through the play is good, but sad. There is no divertissement or tank in it, but the funeral more than makes up for all that.

Where Portia begs Brutus, before the assassination, to tell her all and let her in on the ground floor, and asks what the matter is, and he claims that it is malaria, and she still insists and asks, "Dwell I but in the suburbs of your good pleasure?" and he states, "You are my true and honorable wife, as dear to me as are the ruddy drops that visit my sad heart," I forgot myself and wept my new plug hat two-thirds full. It is as good as anything there is in Josh Whitcomb's play.

Booth and Barrett have the making of good actors in them. I met both of these gentlemen in Wyoming some years ago. We met by accident. They were going to California and I was coming back. By some oversight we had both selected the same track, and we were thrown together. I do not know whether they will recall my face or not. I was riding on the sleeper truck at the time of the accident. I always take a sleeper and always did. I rode on the truck because I didn't want to ride inside the car and have to associate with a wealthy porter who looked down upon me. I am the man who was found down the creek the next day gathering wild ferns and murmuring, "Where am I?"

The play of "Julius Caesar" is one which brings out the meanness and magnetism of Cassius, and emphasizes the mistaken patriotism of Brutus. It is full of pathos, duplicity, assassination, treachery, erroneous loyalty, suicide, hypocrisy, and all the intrigue, jealousy, cowardice and deviltry which characterized the politics of fifty years B.C., but which now, thanks to the enlightenment and refinement which twenty centuries have brought, are known no more forever. Let us not forget, as we enter upon the year 1888, that it is a Presidential year, and that all acrimony will be buried under the dew and the daisies, and that no matter how high party spirit may run, there will be no personal enmity.

(*Nye and Riley's Railway Guide*, 1888)

The Youmorist

"You are an youmorist, are you not?" queried a long-billed pelican addressing a thoughtful, mental athlete, on the Milwaukee & St. Paul road the other day.

"Yes, sir," said the sorrowful man, brushing away a tear. "I am an youmorist. I am not very much so, but still I can see that I am drifting that way. And yet I was once joyous and happy as you are. Only a few years ago, before I was exposed to this malady, I was as blithe as a speckled yearling, and recked not of aught—nor anything else, either. Now my whole life is blasted. I do not dare to eat pie or preserves, and no one tells funny stories when I am near. They regard me as a professional, and when I get in sight the 'scrub nine' close up and wait for me to entertain the crowd and waddle around the ring."

"What do you mean by that?" murmured the purple-nosed interrogation point.

"Mean? Why, I mean that whether I'm drawing a salary or not, I'm expected to be the 'life of the party.' I don't want to be the life of the party. I want to let some one else be the life of the party. I want to get up the reputation of being as cross as a bear with a sore head. I want people to watch their children for fear I'll swallow them. I want to take my low-cut-evening-dress smile and put it in the bureau drawer, and tell the world I've got a cancer in my stomach, and the heaves and hypochondria, and a malignant case of leprosy."

"Do you mean to say that you do not feel facetious all the time, and that you get weary of being an youmorist?"

"Yes, hungry interlocutor. Yes, low-browed students, yes. I am not always tickled. Did you ever have a large, angry, and abnormally protuberant boil somewhere on your person where it seemed to be in the way? Did you ever have such a boil as a traveling companion, and then get introduced to people as an youmorist? You have not? Well, then, you do not know all there is of suffering in this sorrow-streaked world. When wealthy people die why don't they endow a cast-iron castle with a draw-bridge to it and call it the youmorists' retreat? Why don't they do some good with their money instead of fooling it away on those who are comparatively happy?"

"But how did you come to git to be an youmorist?"

"Well, I don't know. I blame my parents some. They might have prevented it if they'd taken it in time, but they didn't. They let it run on till it got established, and now it's no use to go to the Hot Springs or to the mountains, or have an operation performed. You let a man get the name of being an youmorist and he doesn't dare to register at the hotels, and he has to travel anonymously, and mark his clothes with his wife's name, or the public will lynch him if he doesn't say something youmorous.

"Where is your boy to-night?" continued the gloomy humorist. "Do you know where he is? Is he at home under your watchful eye, or is he away somewhere nailing the handles on his first little joke? Parent, beware. Teach your boy to beware. Watch him night and day, or all at once, when he is beyond your jurisdiction, he will grow pale. He will have a far-away look in his eye, and the bright, rosy lad will have become the flat-chested, joyless youmorist.

"It's hard to speak unkindly of our parents, but mingled with my own remorse I shall always murmur to myself, and ask over and over, why did not my parents rescue me while they could? Why did they allow my chubby little feet to waddle down to the dangerous ground on which the sad-eyed youmorist must forever stand?

"Partner, do not forget what I have said to-day. Whether your child be a son or daughter, it matters not. Discourage the first sign of approaching humor. It is easier to bust the backbone of the first little, tender jokelet that sticks its head through the virgin soil, than it is to allow the slimy folds of your son's youmorous lecture to be wrapped about you, and to bring your gray hairs with sorrow to the grave."

(*Baled Hay*, 1884)

Foreign Opinion

We are indebted to Fred J. Prouting, correspondent of the foreign and British newspaper press, for a copy of the London *Daily News* of the 9th inst., containing the following editorial notice:

"If ever celebrity were attained unexpectedly, most assuredly it was that thrust upon Bill Nye by Truthful James. It is just possible, however, that the innumerable readers of Mr. Bret Harte's 'Heathen Chinee' may have imagined Bill Nye and Ah Sin to be purely mythical personages. So far as the former is concerned, any such conclusion now appears to have been erroneous. Bill Nye is no more a phantom than any other journalist, although the name of the organ which he 'runs' savors more of fiction than of fact. But there is no doubt about the matter, for the Washington correspondent of the New York *Tribune* telegraphed on the 29th instant that Bill Nye had accepted a post under the government. He has lately been domiciled in Laramie City, Wyoming territory, and is editor of *The Daily Boomerang*. In reference to Acting-Postmaster-Gen. Hatton's appointment of him as postmaster at Laramie City, the opponent of Ah Sin writes an extremely humorous letter, 'extending' his thanks, and advising his chief of his opinion that his 'appointment is a triumph of eternal truth over error and wrong.' Nye continues: 'It is one of the epochs, I may say, in the nation's onward march toward political purity and perfection. I don't know when I have noticed any stride in the affairs of state which has so thoroughly impressed me with its wisdom.' In this quiet strain of banter, Bill Nye continues to the end of his letter, which suggests the opinion that whatever the official qualifications of the new postmaster may be, the inhabitants of Laramie City must have a very readable newspaper in *The Daily Boomerang.*"

While thanking our London contemporary for its gentle and harmless remarks, we desire to correct an erroneous impression that the *News* seems to have as to our general style. The British press has in some way arrived at the conclusion that the editor of this fashion-guide and mental lighthouse on the rocky shores of time (terms cash), is a party with wild tangled hair and an eye like a tongue of flame.

That is not the case, and therefore our English co-worker in the great field of journalism is, no doubt, laboring under a popular misapprehension. Could the editor of the *News* look in upon us as we pull down tome after tome of forgotten lore in our study; or, with a glad smile, glance hurriedly over the postal card in transit through our postoffice, he would see, not as he supposes, a wild and cruel slayer of his fellow men, but a thoughtful, scholarly and choice fragment of modern architecture, with lines of care about the firmly chiseled mouth, and with the subdued and chastened air of a man who has run for the legislature and failed to get there, Eli.

The London *News* is an older paper than ours, and we therefore recognize the value of its kind notice. *The Boom-*

erang is a young paper, and has therefore only begun fairly to do much damage as a national misfortune, but the time is not far distant, when, from Greenland's icy moutains to India's coral strand, we propose to search out suffering humanity and make death easier and more desirable, by introducing this choice malady.

Regarding the postoffice, we wish to state that we shall aim to make it a great financial success, and furnish mail at all times to all who desire it, whether they have any or not. We shall be pretty busy, of course, attending to the office during the day, and writing scathing editorials during the night, but we will try to snatch a moment now and then to write a few letters for those who have been inquiring sadly and hopelessly for letters during the past ten years. It is, indeed, a dark and dreary world to the man who has looked in at the same general delivery window nine times a day for ten years, and yet never received a letter, nor even a confidential postal card from a commercial man, stating that on the 5th of the following month he would strike the town with a new and attractive line of samples.

We should early learn to find out such suffering as that, and if we are in the postoffice department we may be the means of much good by putting new envelopes on our own dunning letters and mailing them to the suffering and distressed. Let us, in our abundance, remember those who have not been dunned for many a weary year. It will do them good, and we will not feel the loss.

(*Baled Hay*, 1884)

English Humor

The London *Spectator* says that "the humor of the United States, if closely examined, will be found to depend in a great measure on the ascendancy which the principle of utility has gained over the imaginations of a rather imaginative people." The humor of England, if closely examined, will be found just about ready to drop over the picket fence into the arena, but never quite making connections. If we scan the English literary horizon, we will find the humorist up a tall tree, depending from a sharp knot thereof by the slack of his overalls. He is just out of sight at the time you look in that direction. He always has a man working in his place, however. The man who works in his place is just paring down the half sole, and newly pegging a joke, that has recently been sent in by the foreman for repairs.

(*Baled Hay*, 1884)

The English Joke

The average English joke has its peculiarities. A sort of mellow distance. A kind of chastened reluctance. A coy and timid, yet trusting, though evanescent intangibility which softly lingers in the untroubled air, and lulls the tired senses to dreamy rest, like the subdued murmur of a hoarse jackass about nine miles up the gulch.

He must be a hardened wretch, indeed, who has not felt his bosom heave and the scalding tear steal down his furrowed cheek after he has read an English joke. There can be no hope for the man who has not been touched by the gentle, pleading, yet all potent sadness embodied in the humorous paragraph of the true Englishman.

(*Bill Nye's Chestnuts, Old and New*, 1887)

The Newspaper

An address delivered before the Wisconsin State Press Association, at Whitewater, Wis., August 11, 1885

Mr. President and Gentlemen of the Press of Wisconsin:

I am sure that when you so kindly invited me to address you today, you did not anticipate a lavish display of genius and gestures. I accepted the invitation because it afforded me an opportunity to meet you and to get acquainted with you and tell you personally that for years I have been a constant reader of your valuable paper and I like it. You are running it just as I like to see a newspaper run.

I need not elaborate upon the wonderful growth of the press in our country or refer to the great power which journalism wields in the development of the new world. I need not ladle out statistics to show you how the newspaper has encroached upon the field of oratory and how the pale and silent man, while others sleep, compiles the universal history of a day and tells his mighty audience what he thinks about it before he goes to bed.

Of course, this is but the opinion of one man, but who has a better opportunity to judge than he who sits with his finger on the electric pulse of the world, judging the actions of humanity at so much per judge, invariably in advance?

I need not tell you all this, for you certainly know it if you read your paper, and I hope you do. A man ought to read his own paper, even if he cannot endorse all its sentiments.

So necessary has the profession of journalism become to the progress and education of our country, that the matter of establishing schools where young men may be fitted for an active newspaper life has attracted much attention and discussion. It has been demonstrated that our colleges do not fit a young man to walk at once into the active management of a paper. He should at least know the difference between a vile contemporary and a Gothic scoop.

It is difficult to map out a proper course for the student in a school of journalism, there are so many things connected with the profession which the editor and his staff should know and know hard. The newspaper of today is a library. It is an encyclopaedia, a poem, a biography, a history, a prophecy, a directory, a time-table, a romance, a cook book, a guide, a horoscope, an art critic, a political resume, a *multum in parvo*. It is a sermon, a song, a circus, an obituary, a picnic, a shipwreck, a symphony in a solid brevier, a medley of life and death, a grand aggregation of man's glory and his shame. It is, in short, a bird's-eye-view of all the magnanimity and meanness, the joys and griefs, the births and deaths, the pride and poverty of the world, and all for two cents—sometimes.

I could tell you some more things that the newspaper of today is if you had time to stay here and your business would not suffer in your absence. Among others it is a long felt want, a nine-column paper in a five-column town, a lying sheet, a feeble effort, a financial problem, a tottering wreck, a political tool and a sheriff's sale.

If I were to suggest a curriculum for the young man who wished to take a regular course in a school of journalism, preferring that to the actual experience, I would say to him, devote the first two years to meditation and prayer. This will prepare the young editor for the surprise and consequent temptation to profanity which in a few years he may experience when he finds that the name of the Deity in his double-leaded editorial is spelled with a little "g," and the peroration of the article is locked up between a death notice and the advertisement of a patent moustache coaxer, which is to follow pure reading matter every day in the week and occupy the top of column on Sunday tf.*

*An old journalistic expression meaning "to follow."—Ed.

The ensuing five years should be devoted to the peculiar orthography of the English language.

Then put in three years with the dumb bells, sand bags, slung shots and tomahawk. In my own journalistic experience I have found more cause for regret over my neglect of this branch than anything else. I usually keep on my desk during a heated campaign a large paper weight weighing three or four pounds, and in several instances I have found that I could feed that to a constant reader of my valuable paper instead of a retraction.

Fewer people lick the editor though, now, than did so in years gone by. Many people—in the last two years—have gone across the street to lick the editor and never returned. They intended to come right back in a few moments, but they are now in a land where a change of heart and a palm leaf fan is all they need.

Fewer people are robbing the editor nowadays, too, I notice with much pleasure. Only a short time ago I noticed that a burglar succeeded in breaking into the residence of a Dakota journalist, and after a long, hard struggle the editor succeeded in robbing him.

After the primary course, mapped out already, an intermediate course of ten years should be given to learning the typographical art, so that when visitors come in and ask the editor all about the office, he can tell them of the mysteries of making a paper, and how delinquent subscribers have frequently been killed by a well-directed blow with a printer's towel.

Five years should be devoted to a study of the art of proof-reading. In that length of time the young journalist can perfect himself to such a degree that it will take another five years for the printer to understand his corrections and marginal notes.

Fifteen years should then be devoted to the study of American politics, especially civil service reform, looking at it from a non-partisan standpoint. If possible, the last five years should be spent abroad. London is the place to go if you wish to get a clear, concise view of American politics, and Chicago or Milwaukee would be a good place for the young English journalist to go and study the political outlook of England.

The student should then take a medical and surgical course, so that he may be able to attend to contusions, fractures and so forth which may occur to himself or to the party who may come to his office for a retraction and by mistake get his spinal column double-leaded.

Ten years should then be given to the study of law. No thorough, metropolitan editor wants to enter upon the duties of his profession without knowing the difference between a writ of *mandamus* and other styles of profanity. He should thoroughly understand the entire system of American jurisprudence, so that in case a *certiorari* should break out in his neighborhood he would know just what to do for it.

The student will, by this time, begin to see what is required of him and enter with great zeal upon the further study of his profession.

He will now enter upon a theological course of ten years and fit himself thoroughly to speak intelligently of the various creeds and religions of the world. Ignorance on the part of an editor is almost a crime, and when he closes a powerful editorial with the familiar quotation, "It is the early bird that catches the worm," and attributes it to St. Paul instead of Deuteronomy, it makes me blush for the profession.

The last ten years may be profitably devoted to the acquisition of a practical knowledge of cutting cordwood, baking beans, making shirts, lecturing, turning double handsprings, being shot out of a catapult at a circus, learning how to make a good adhesive paste that will not sour in hot weather, grinding scissors, punctuating, capitalization, condemnation, syntax, plain sewing, music and dancing, sculping, etiquette, prosody, how to win the affections of the opposite sex and evade a malignant case of breach of promise, the ten commandments, every man his own tooter on the flute, croquet, rules of the prize ring, rhetoric, parlor magic, calisthenics, penmanship, how to run a jack from the bottom of the pack without getting shot, civil engineering, decorative art, kalsomining, bicycling, baseball, hydraulics, botany, poker, international law, high-low-jack, drawing and painting, faro, vocal music, driving, breaking team, fifteen ball pool, how to remove grease spots from last year's pantaloons, horsemanship, coupling freight cars, riding on a rail, riding on a pass, feeding threshing machines, how to wean a calf from the parent stem, teaching school, bull-whacking, plastering, waltzing, vaccination, autopsy, how to win the affections of your wife's mother, every man his own washerwoman, or how to wash underclothes so they will not shrink, etc., etc.

But time forbids anything like a thorough list of what a young man should study in order to fully understand all that he may be called upon to express an opinion about in his actual experience as a journalist. There are a thousand little matters which every editor should know; such, for instance, as the construction of roller composition. Many newspaper men can write a good editorial on Asiatic cholera, but their roller composition is not fit to eat.

With the course of study that I have mapped out, the young student would emerge from the college of journalism at the age of 95 or 96, ready to take off his coat and write an article on almost any subject. He would be a little giddy at first, and the office boy would have to see that he went to bed at a proper time each night, but aside from that he would be a good man to feed a waste paper basket.

Actual experience is the best teacher in this peculiarly trying profession. I hope some day to attend a press convention where the order of exercise will consist of five-minute experiences from each one present. It would be worth listening to.

My own experience was a little peculiar. It was my intention at first to practice law, when I went to the Rocky Mountains, although I had been warned by the authorities not to do so. Still, I did practice in a surreptitious kind of a way, and might have been practicing yet if my client hadn't died. When you have become attached to a client and respect and like him, and then when, without warning, like a bolt of electricity from a clear sky, he suddenly dies and takes the bread right out of your mouth, it is rough.

Then I tried the practice of criminal law, but my client got into the penitentiary, where he was no use to me financially or politically. Finally, when the judge was in a hurry, he would appoint me to defend the pauper criminals. They all went to the penitentiary, until people got to criticizing the judge, and finally they told him that it was a shame to appoint me to defend an innocent man.

My first experience in journalism was in a Western town in which I was a total stranger. I went there with thirty-five cents, but I had it concealed in the lining of my clothes so that no one would have suspected it if they had met me. I had no friends, and I noticed that when I got off the train the band was not there to meet me. I entered the town just as any other American citizen would. I had not fully decided whether to become a stage robber or a lecturer on phrenology. At that time I got a chance to work on a morning paper. It used to go to press before dark, so I always had my evenings to myself and I liked that part of it first-rate. I worked on that paper a year and might have continued if the proprietors had not changed it to an evening paper.

Then a company incorporated itself and started a paper, of which I took charge. The paper was published in the loft of a livery stable. That is the reason they called it a stock company. You could come up the stairs into the office or you could twist the tail of the iron-gray mule and take the elevator.

It wasn't much of a paper, but it cost $16,000 a year to run it, and it came out six days in the week no matter what the weather was. We took the Associated Press news by telegraph part of the time, and part of the time we relied on the Cheyenne morning papers, which we got of the conductor on the early morning freight. We got a great many special telegrams from Washington in that way, and when the freight train got in late I had to guess at what congress was doing and fix up a column of telegraph the best I could. There was a rival evening paper there, and sometimes it would send a smart boy down to the train and get hold of our special telegrams, and sometimes the conductor would go away on a picnic and take our Cheyenne paper with him.

All these things are annoying to a man who is trying to supply a long felt want. There was one conductor, in particular, who used to go away into the foothills shooting sage hens and take our cablegrams with him. This threw too much strain on me. I could guess at what congress was doing and make up a pretty readable report, but foreign powers and reichstags and crowned heads and dynasties always mixed me up. You can look over what congress did last year and give a pretty good guess at what it will do this year, but you can't rely on a dynasty or an effete monarchy in a bad state of preservation. It may go into executive session or it may go into bankruptcy.

Still, at one time we used to have considerable local news to fill up with. The north and middle parks for a while used to help us out when the mining camps were new. Those were the days when it was considered perfectly proper to kill off the board of supervisors if their action was distasteful. At that time a new camp generally located a cemetery and wrote an obituary; then the boys would start out to find a man whose name would rhyme with the rest of the verse. Those were the days when the cemeteries of Colorado were still in their infancy and the song of the six-shooter was heard in the land.

Sometimes the Indians would send us in an item. It was generally in the obituary line. With the Sioux on the north and the peaceful Utes on the south, we were pretty sure of some kind of news during the summer. The parks used to be occupied by white men winters and Indians summers. Summer was really the pleasantest time to go into the parks, but the Indians had been in the habit of going there at that season, and they were so clannish that the white men couldn't have much fun with them, so they decided they would not go there in the summer. Several of our best subscribers were killed by the peaceful Utes.

There were two daily and three weekly papers published in Laramie City at that time. There were between two and three thousand people and our local circulation ran from 150 to 250, counting dead-heads. In our prospectus we stated that we would spare no expense whatever in ransacking the universe for fresh news, but there were times when it was all we could do to get our paper out on time. Out of the express office, I mean.

One of the rival editors used to write his editorials for the paper in the evening, jerk the Washington hand-press to work them off, go home and wrestle with juvenile colic in his family until daylight and then deliver his papers on the street. It is not surprising that the great mental strain incident to this life made an old man of him, and gave a tinge of extreme sadness to the funny column of his paper.

In an unguarded moment, this man wrote an editorial once that got all his subscribers mad at him, and the same afternoon he came around and wanted to sell his paper to us for $10,000. I told him that the whole outfit wasn't worth ten thousand cents.

"I know that," said he, "but it is not the material that I am talking about. It is the good will of the paper."

We had a rising young horse thief in Wyoming in those days, who got into jail by some freak of justice, and it was so odd for a horse thief to get into jail that I alluded to it editorially. This horse thief had distinguished himself from the common, vulgar horse thieves of his time, by wearing a large mouth—a kind of full-dress, eight-day mouth. He rarely smiled, but when he did, he had to hold the top of his head on with both hands. I remember that I spoke of this in the paper, forgetting that he might criticize me when he got out of jail. When he did get out again, he stated that he would shoot me on sight, but friends advised me not to have his blood on my hands, and I took their advice, so I haven't got a particle of his blood on either of my hands.

For two or three months I didn't know but he would drop into the office any minute and criticize me, but one day a friend told me that he had been hung in Montana. Then I began to mingle in society again, and didn't have to get in my coal with a double barrel shotgun any more.

After that I was always conservative in relation to horse thieves until we got the report of the vigilance committee.

(*Bill Nye's Remarks*, 1887)

Requesting a Remittance

[Personal]

Washington, D. C.
Along toward morning, 1887.

Cashier World Office, New York.—

My dear sir: You will doubtless be surprised to hear from me so soon, as I did not promise when I left New York that I would write you at all while here. But now I take pen in hand to say that the Senate and House of Representatives are having a good deal of fun with me, and hope you are enjoying the same great blessing. You will wonder at first why I send in my expense account before I send in anything for the paper, but I will explain that to you when I get back. At first I thought I would not bother with the expense account till I got to your office, but I can now see that it is going to worry me to get there unless I hear from you favorably by return mail.

When I came here I fell into the mad whirl of society, and attracted a good deal of attention by my cultivated ways and Jeffersonian method of sleeping with a different member of Congress every night.

I have not written anything for publication yet, but I am

getting material together that will make people throughout our broad land open their eyes in astonishment. I shall deal fairly and openly with these great national questions, and frankly hew to the line, let the chips fall where they may, as I heard a man say to-day on the floor of the house—the Willard House, I mean. But I believe in handling great political matters without gloves, as you will remember, if you have watched my course as justice of the peace and litterateur. Candor is my leading characteristic, and if you will pardon me for saying so in the first letter you ever received from me I believe there is nothing about my whole character which seems to challenge my admiration for myself any more than that.

Congressmen and their wives are daily landing at the great national Castle Garden and looking wildly around for the place where they are told they will get their mileage. On every hand all is hurry and excitement. Bills are being introduced, acquaintances renewed, and punch bowls are beginning to wear a preoccupied air.

I have been mingling with society ever since I came here, and that is one reason I have written very little for publication, and did not send what I did write.

Yesterday afternoon my money gave out at 3:20, and since that my mind has been clearer and society has made fewer demands on me. At first I thought I would obtain employment at the Treasury Department as exchange editor in the greenback room. Then I remembered that I would get very faint before I could go through a competitive examination, and, in the meantime, I might lose social caste by wearing my person on the outside of my clothes. So I have resolved to write you a chatty letter about Washington, assuring you that I am well, and asking you kindly to consider the enclosed tabulated bill of expenses, as I need the money to buy Christmas presents and get home with.

Poker is one of the curses of national legislation. I have several times heard prominent foreigners say, in their own language—thinking, no doubt, that I could not understand them—that the members of the American Congress did not betray any emotion on their countenances. One foreigner from Liverpool, who thought I could not understand his language, said that our congressmen had a way of looking as though they did not know very much. When he afterwards played poker with those same men he saw that the look was acquired. One man told me that his vacant look had been as good as $50,000 to him, whether he stood pat or drew to an ostensible flush while really holding four bullets.

So far I have not been over to the Capitol, preferring to have Congress kind of percolate into my room, two or three at a time; but unless you can honor the inclosed way-bill I shall be forced to go over to the House to-morrow and write something for the paper. Since I have been writing this I have been led to inquire whether it would be advisable for me to remain here through the entire session or not. It will be unusually long, lasting perhaps clear into July, and I find that the stenographers as a general thing get a pretty accurate and spicy account of the proceedings, much more so than I can, and as you will see by inclosed statement it is going to cost more to keep me here than I figured on.

My idea was that board and lodgings would be the main items of expense, but I struck a low-priced place, where, by clubbing together with some plain gentlemen from a distance who have been waiting here three years for political recognition, and who do not feel like surrounding themselves with a hotel, we get a plain room with six beds in it. The room overlooks the District of Columbia, and the first man in has the choice of beds, with the privilege of inviting friends to a limited number. We lunch plainly in the lower part of the building in a standing position without restraint or finger-bowls. So board is not the principal item of expense, though of course I do not wish to put up at a place where I will be a disgrace to the paper.

I wish that you would, when you send my check, write me frankly whether you think I had better remain here during the entire season or not. I like the place first rate, but my duties keep me up nights to a late hour, and I cannot sleep during the day, because my roommates annoy me by doing their washing and ironing over an oil stove.

I know by what several friends have said to me that Congress would like to have me stay here all winter, but I want to do what is best for the paper.

I saw Mr. Cleveland briefly last evening at his home, but he was surrounded by a crowd of fawning sycophants, so I did not get a chance to speak to him as I would like to, and don't know as he would have advanced the amount to me anyway. He is very firm and stubborn, I judged, and would yield very little indeed, especially to

Yours truly,
Bill Nye.

The following bill looks large in the aggregate, but when you come to examine each item by itself there is really nothing startling about it, and when you remember that I have been here now four days and that this is the first bill I have sent in to the office during that time, I know you will not consider it out of the way, especially as you are interested in seeing me make a good paper of the *World*, no matter what the expense is.

We are having good open winter weather and stock is looking well so far.

I fear you will regard the item for embalming as exorbitant, and it is so, but I was compelled to pay that price, as the man had to be shipped a long distance, and I did not want to shock his friends too much when he met them at the depot.

To rent of dress suit for the purpose of seeing life in Washington in the interest of the paper	$4.50
To charges for dispersing turtle soup from lap of same	1.00
To getting fur collar put on overcoat, in interest of paper	9.00
To amount loaned a gentleman who had lived in Washington a long time and could make me a social	

pet (I will return same to you in case he pays it before I come back)	5.00
To lodgings two nights at 25 cents	.50
Six meals at 15 cents.	.90
Pen and ink	.20
Postage on this letter	.08
Bronchial troches, in interest of paper	.20
Car fare	.60
Laundry work done in interest of paper	.30
Carriage hire in getting from humble home of a senator to my own voluptuous lodgings.	2.00
To expenses of embalming a man who came to me and wanted me to use my influence in changing policy of the paper	180.00
To fine paid for assault and battery in and upon a gentleman who said he wanted my influence, but really was already under other influence, and who stepped on my stomach twice without offering to apologize	19.00
Paid janitor of jail next morning	1.00
Paid for breaking the window of my cell	.50
Paid damage for writing humorous poetry on wall of cell so that it could not be erased	2.00
Total	$226.78

I will probably remain here until I hear from you favorably. I have met several members of Congress for whom I have voted at various times off and on, but they were cold and haughty in their intercourse with me. I have been invited to sit on the floor of the House until I get some other place to stay, but I hate to ride a free horse to death.

(*Bill Nye's Thinks*, 1888)

The Drug Business in Kansas

Hudson, Wis.

Mr. Bill Nye.—Dear Sir: I hope you will pardon me for addressing you on a matter of pure business, but I have heard that you are not averse to going out of your way to do a favor now and then to those who are sincere and appreciative.

I have learned from a friend that you have been around all over the west, and so I have taken the liberty of writing you to ask what you think would be the chances of success for a young man if he were to go to Kansas to enter the drug business.

I am a practical young druggist 23 years of age and have some money—a few hundred dollars—with which to go into business. Would you advise Kansas or Colorado as a good part of the west for that business?

I have also written some for the press but with little success. I inclose you a few slips cut from the papers in which these articles originally appeared. I send stamp for reply and hope you will answer me, even though your time may be taken up pretty well by other matters. Respectfully yours,

ADOLPH JAYNES, Lock-Box 604.

Hudson, Wis., Oct. 1.

Mr. Adolph Jaynes, Lock-box 604.—

Dear Sir: Your favor of late date is at hand, and I take pleasure in writing this dictated letter to you, using the columns of the Chicago *Daily News* as a delicate way of teaching you. I will take the liberty of replying to your last question first, if you pardon me, and I say that you would do better, no doubt at once, in a financial way, to go on with your drug business than to monkey with literature.

In the first place your style of composition is like the present style of dress among men. It is absolutely correct, and therefore it is absolutely like that of nine men out of every ten we meet. Your style of writing has a mustache on it, wears a three-button cutaway of some Scotch mixture, carries a cane, and wears a straight, stand-up collar and scarf. It is so correct and so exactly in conformity with the prevailing style of composition, and your thoughts are expressed so thoroughly like other people's methods of dressing up their sentences and sand-papering the soul out of what they say, that I honestly think you would succeed better by trying to subsist upon the quick sales and small profits which the drug trade insures.

Now, let us consider the question of location.

Seriously, you ought to look over the ground yourself, but as you have asked me to give you my best judgment on the question of preference as between Kansas and Colorado I will say without hesitation that, if you mean by the drug business the sale of sure-enough drugs, medicines, paints, oils, glass, putty, toilet articles, and prescriptions carefully compounded, I would *not* go to Kansas at this time.

If you would like to go to a flourishing country and put out a big basswood mortar in front of your shop in order to sell the tincture of damnation throughout bleeding Kansas, now is your golden opportunity. Now is the accepted time. If it is the great, big, burning desire of your heart to go into a town of 2,000 people and open the thirteenth drug store in order that you may stand behind a tall black-walnut prescription case day in and day out, with a graduate in one hand and a Babcock fire-extinguisher in the other, filling orders for whisky made of stump-water and the juice of future punishment, you will do well to go to Kansas. It is a temperance state, and no saloons are allowed there. All is quiet and orderly, and the drug business is a great success.

You can run a dummy drug store there with two dozen

dreary old glass bottles on the shelves, punctuated by the hand of time and the Kansas fly of the period, and with a prohibitory law at your back and a tall, red barrel in the back room filled with a mixture that will burn great holes into nature's heart and make the cemetery blossom as the rose, and in a few years you can sell enough of this justly celebrated preparation for household, scientific, and experimental purposes only to fill your flabby pockets with wealth and paint the pure air of Kansas a bright and inflammatory red.

If you sincerely and earnestly yearn for a field where you may go forth and garner an honest harvest from the legitimate effort of an upright soda fountain and free and open sale of slippery elm in its unadulterated condition, I would go to some state where I would not have to enter into competition with a style of pharmacy that has the unholy instincts and ambitions of a blind pig. I would not go into the field where red-eyed ruin simply waited for a prescription blank, not necessarily for publication, but simply as a guaranty of good faith, in order that it may bound forth from behind the prescription case and populate the poor-houses and the paupers' nettle-grown addition to the silent city of the dead.

The great question of how best to down the demon rum is before the American people, and it will not be put aside until it is settled; but while this is being attended to, Mr. Jaynes, I would start a drug store farther away from the center of conflict and go on joyously, sacrificing expensive tinctures, compounds, and sirups at bed-rock prices.

Go on, Mr. Jaynes, dealing out to the yearning, panting public, drugs, paints, oils, glass, putty, varnish, patent medicines, and prescriptions carefully compounded, with none to molest or make afraid, but shun, oh shun the wild-eyed pharmacopoeia that contains naught but the festering fluid so popular in Kansas, a compound that holds crime in solution and ruin in bulk, that shrivels up a man's gastric economy, and sears great ragged holes into his immortal soul. Take this advice home to your heart and you will ever command the hearty co-operation of "yours for health," as the late Lydia E. Pinkham so succinctly said.

(*Bill Nye's Thinks*, 1888)

The Ambrosia of James Whitcomb Riley

"Chelifer" in "The Bookery."—Godoy's Magazine

There are writers that take Pegasus on giddier flights of fancy, and writers that sit him more grandly, and writers that put him through daintier paces, and writers that burden him with anguish nearer that of the dread Rider of the White Horse, and there are writers that make him a very bucking broncho of wit, but there is no one that turns Pegasus into just such an ambling nag of lazy peace and pastoral content as James—I had almost said Joshua Whitcomb—Riley. If you want a panacea for the bitterness and the fret and the snobbishness and pretension and unsympathy and the commercial ambition and worry and the other cankers that gnaw and gnaw the soul, just throw a leg over the back of Riley's Pegasus, "perfectly safe for family driving," let the reins hang loose as you sag limply in your saddle, and gaze through drowsy eyes while the amiable old beast jogs down lanes blissful with rural quietude, through farmyards full of picturesque rustics and through the streets of quaint villages. Then utter rest and a peace akin to bliss will possess your soul.

To make readers content with life and glad to live is one of the most dazzlingly magnificent deeds in the power of an artist. This is too little appreciated in the melodramatic theatricism of our life. This genius for soothing the reader with a pathos that is not anguish and a humor that is not cynicism, this genius belongs to Mr. Riley in a degree I have found in no ther writer in all literature.

Of course, Mr. Riley is essentially a lyric poet. But his spirit is that of Walt Whitman; he speaks the universal democracy, the equality of man, the hatred of assumption and snobbery, that our republic stands for, if it stands for anything. Now downright didacticism in a poet is an abomination. But if a poet has no right to ponder the meanings of things, the feelings of man for man and the higher "criticism of life," then no one has. If to Pope's "The proper study of mankind is man," you add "nature" and "nature's God," you will fairly well outline the poet's field.

Mere art (Heaven save the "mere"!) is not, and has never been, enough to place a poet among the great spirits of the world. It has furnished a number of nimble mandolinists and exquisite dilettantes for lazy moods. But great poetry must always be something more than sweetmeats; it must be food—temptingly cooked, winningly served, well spiced and well accompanied, but yet food to strengthen the blood and the sinews of the soul.

Therefore I make so bold as to insist that even in a lyrist there should be something more than the prosperity or the dirge of personal *amours*: there should be a sympathy with the world-joy, the world-suffering, and the world-kinship. It is this attitude toward lyric poetry that makes me think Mr. Riley a poet whose exquisite art is lavished on humanity so deep-sounding as to commend him to the acceptance of immortality among the highest lyrists.

Horace was an acute thinker and a frank speaker on the problems of life. This didacticism seems not to have harmed his artistic welfare, for he has undoubtedly been the most popular poet that ever wrote. Consider the magnitude and the enthusiasm of his audience! He has been the personal chum of everyone that ever read Latinity. But Horace, when not exalted with his inspired preachments on the art of life and the arts of poetry and love, was a bitter cynic redeemed by great self-depreciation and joviality. The son of a slave, he was too fond of court life to talk democracy.

Bobby Burns was a thorough child of the people and is

more like Mr. Riley in every way than any other poet. Yet he, too, had a vicious cynicism, and he never had the polished art that enriches some of Mr. Riley's non-dialectic poetry, as in parts of his fairy fancy, "The Flying Islands of the Night."

Burns never had the versatility of sympathy that enables Mr. Riley to write such unpastoral masterpieces as "Anselmo," "The Dead Lover," "A Scrawl," "The Home-going," some of his sonnets, and the noble verses beginning.

> "A momument for the soldiers!
> And what will ye build it of?"

Yet it must be owned that Burns is in general Mr. Riley's prototype. Mr. Riley admits it himself in his charming verses "To Robert Burns."

> "Sweet singer, that I lo'e the maist
> O' ony, sin' wi' eager haste
> I smacket bairn lips ower the taste
> O' hinnied sang."

The classic pastoral poets, Theokritos, Vergandil, the others, sang with an exquisite art, indeed, yet their farm-folk were really Dresden-china shepherds and shepherdesses speaking with affected simplicity or with impossible elegance. Theokritos, like Burns and Riley, wrote partly in dialect and partly in the standard speech, and to those who are never reconciled to anything that can quote no "authority," there should be sufficient justification for dialect poetry in this divine Sicilian musician of whom his own Goatherd might have said:

> "Full of fine honey thy beautiful mouth was, Thyrsis, created—
> Full of the honeycomb; figs Aegilean, too, mayest thou nibble,
> Sweet as they are; for ev'n than the locust more bravely thou singest."

I have no room to argue the *pro's* of dialect here, but it always seems strange that those lazy critics who are unwilling to take the trouble to translate the occasional hard words in a dialect form of their own tongue, should be so inconsistent as ever to study a foreign language. Then, too, dialect is necessary to truth, to local color, to intimacy with the character depicted. Besides, it is delicious. There is something mellow and soul-warming about a plebeian metathesis like "congergation." What orthoepy could replace lines like these?:

> "Worter, shade and all so mixed, don't know which you'd orter
> Say, th' *worter* in the shadder—*shadder* in the worter!"

One thing about Mr. Riley's dialect that may puzzle those not familiar with the living speech of the Hoosiers is his spelling, which is chiefly done as if by the illiterate speaker himself. thus "rostneer-time" and "ornry" must be Aeolic Greek to those barbarians who have never heard of "roasting-ears" of corn or of that contemptuous synonym for "vulgar," "common," which is smoothly elided, "or(di)n(a)ry." Both of these words could be spelled with a suggestive and helpful use of apostrophes: "roast'n'-ear," and "or'n'ry."

Jumbles like "jevver" for "did you ever?" and the like can hardly be spelled otherwise than phonetically, but a glossary should be appended as in Lowell's "Biglow Papers," for the poems are eminently worth even lexicon-thumbing. Another frequent fault of dialect writers is the spelling phonetically of words pronounced everywhere alike. Thus "enough" is spelled "enuff," and "clamor," "clammer," though Dr. Johnson himself would never have pronounced them otherwise. In these misspellings, however, Mr. Riley excuses himself by impersonating an illiterate as well as a crude-speaking poet. But even then he is inconsistent, and "hollowing" becomes "hollerin'," with an apostrophe to mark the lost "g"—that abominable imported harshness that ought to be generally exiled from our none too smooth language. Mr. Riley has written a good essay in defense of dialect, which enemies of this form of literature might read with advantage.

But Mr. Riley has written a deal of most excellent verse that is not in dialect. One whole volume is devoted to a fairy extravaganza called "The Flying Islands of the Night," a good addition to that quaint literature of lace to which "The Midsummer Night's Dream," Herrick's "Oberon's Epithalamium," or whatever it is called, Drake's "Culprit Fay," and other bits of most exquisite foolery belong. While hardly a complete success, this diminutive drama contains some curiously delightful conceits like this "improvisation":

"Her face—her brow—her hair unfurled!—
And O the oval chin below,
Carved, like a cunning cameo,
With one exquisite dimple, swirled
With swimming shine and shade, and whirled
The daintiest vortex poets know—
The sweetest whirlpool ever twirled
By Cupid's finger-tip—and so,
The deadliest maelstrom in the world!"

It is a strange individuality that Mr. Riley has, suggesting numerous other masters—whose influence he acknowledges in special odes—and yet all digested and assimilated into a marked individuality of his own. He has studied the English poets profoundly and improved himself upon them, till one is chiefly impressed, in his non-dialectic verse, with his refinement, subtlety, and ease. He has a large vocabulary, and his felicity is at times startling. Thus he speaks of water "chuckling," which is as good as Horace's ripples that "gnaw" the shore. Note the mastery of such lines as

"And the dust of the road is like velvet."

"Nothin' but green woods and clear
Skies and unwrit poetry
By the acre!"

"Then God smiled and it was morning!"

"Life is "A poor pale yesterday of Death."

"And O I wanted so
To be felt sorry for!"

"Always suddenly they are gone,
The friends we trusted and held secure."

"At utter loaf."

"Knee-deep in June."

—But I can not go on quoting forever.

Technically, Mr. Riley is a master of surpassing finish. His meters are perfect and varied. They flow as smoothly as his own Indiana streams. His rimes are almost never imperfect. To prove his own understanding he has written one *scherzo* in technic that's a delightful example of bad rime, bad meter, and the other earmarks of the poor poet. It is "Ezra House," and begins:

"Come listen, good people, while a story I do tell
Of the sad fate of one I knew so passing well!"

The "do" and the "so" are the unfailing index of crudity. Then we have rimes like "long" and along" (it is curious that modern English is the only tongue that finds this repetition objectionable); "moon" and "tomb," "well" and "hill," and "said" and "denied" are others, and the whole thing is an enchanting lesson in How Poetry Should Not be Written.

Mr. Riley is fond of dividing words at the ends of lines, but always in a comic way, though Horace, you remember, was not unwilling to use it seriously, as in his

" ——U-
Xorius amnis."

Mr. Riley's animadversions on "Addeliney Bowersox" constitute a fascinating study in this effect. He is also devoted to dividing an adjective from its noun by a line-end. This is a trick of Poe's, whose influence Mr. Riley has greatly profited by. In his dialect poetry Mr. Riley gets just the effect of the jerky drawl of the Hoosier by using the end of a line as a knife, thus:

"The wood's
Green again, and sun feels good's
June!"

His masterly use of the caesura is notable, too. See its charming despotism in "Griggsby Station."

But it is not his technic that makes him ambrosial, not the loving care *ad unguem* that smooths the uncouthest dialect into lilting tunefulness without depriving it of its colloquial verisimilitude—it is none of these things of mechanical inspiration, but the spirit of the man, his democracy, his tenderness, the health and wealth of his sympathies. If he uses "memory" a little too often as a vehicle for his rural pictures, the utter charm of the pictures is atonement enough. He has caught the real American. He is the laureate of the bliss of laziness. His child poems are the next best thing to the child itself; they have all the infectious essence of gayety, and all the *naïveté*, and all the knife-like appeal. It could not reasonably be demanded that his prose should equal the perfection of his verse, but nothing more eerie has ever been done than the little story, "Where is Mary Alice Smith?" with its strange use of rime at the end.

Of all dialect writers he has been the most versatile. Think of the author of "The Raggedy Man" or "Orphant Annie" writing one of the finest sonnets in the language! this one which I must quote here as a noble ending to my halt praise:

"Being his mother, when he goes away
I would not hold him overlong, and so
Sometimes my yielding sight of him grows O
So quick of tears, I joy he did not stay
To catch the faintest rumor of them! Nay,
Leave always his eyes clear and glad, although
Mine own, dear Lord, do fill to overflow;
Let his remembered features, as I pray,
Smile over on me. Ah! what stress of love
Thou givest me to guard with Thee thiswise:
Its fullest speech ever to be denied

Mine own—being his mother! All thereof
Thou knowest only looking from the skies
As when not Christ alone was crucified."

Life is the more tolerable, the more full of learned sympathy, and thereby of joy and value, for the very existence of such a man.

(*A Guest at the Ludlow*, 1897)

CHAPTER *6*

The Woman Question

The Gentle Power of a Woman's Influence

Cummins City is still a crude metropolis.

Society has not yet arrived at the white vest and lawn sociable period there. There is nothing to hamper any one or throw a tiresome restraint around him. You walk up and down the streets of the camp without feeling that the vigilant eye of the policeman is upon you, and when you register at the leading hotel the proprietor don't ask how much baggage you have, or insist upon it that your valise ought to be blown up with a quill to give it a robust appearance.

Speaking of this hotel, however, brings to my mind a little incident which really belongs in here. There are two ladies at this place, the only ones in the city limits, if my memory serves me. One of these ladies owns a lot of poles or house logs which were, at the time of which I speak, on the dump, as it were, ready to be used in the construction of a new cabin.

It seems that some of the prospectors of the corporation, without the fear of God or the Common Council of Cummins City, had been appropriating these logs from time to time until out of a good, fair assortment there remained only a dejected little pile of "culls." The owner had watched with great annoyance the gradual disappearance of her property from day to day, and it made her lose faith in the final redemption of all mankind. She became cynical and misanthropical, lost her interest in the future, and became low spirited and unhappy.

One day, however, after this thing had proceeded about far enough she went to her trunk, taking out the large size of navy revolver, the kind that plows up the vitals so successfully and sends so many Western men to their long home. Then she went out to where a group of men had scattered themselves out around camp to smoke.

She wasn't a large woman at all, but these men respected her. Though they were only rough miners there in the wilderness they recognized that she was a woman, and they recognized it almost at a glance, too. There she was alone among a wild group of men in the mountains, far from the protecting arm of the law and the softening influences of metropolitan life, and yet the common feeling of gallantry implanted in the masculine breast was there.

She indicated with a motion of her revolver that she desired to call the meeting to order. There seemed to be a general anxiety on the part of every man present to come to order just as soon as circumstances would permit. Then she made a short speech relative to the matter of house logs, and suggested that unless a certain number of those articles, now invisible to the naked eye, were placed at a certain point, or a certain amount of kopecks placed on file with the chairman of the meeting within a specified time, that perdition would be popping on Main Street in about two and one-half ticks of the chronometer.

There didn't seem to be any desire on the part of the meeting to amend the motion or lay it on the table. Although it was arbitrary and imperative, and although an opportunity was given for a free expression of opinion, there didn't seem to be any desire to take advantage of it.

A committee of three was appointed to carry out the suggestions of the chair, and in about half an hour, the house logs and kopecks having been placed on deposit at the places designated, the meeting broke up, subject to the call of the chairman.

It was not a very long session, but it was very harmonious—very harmonious and very orderly. There was no calling for the previous question or rising to a point of order. The pale-faced men who composed the convention did not look to the casual observers as though they had come there to raise points for debate over parliamentary practice. They kept their eye on the speaker's desk and didn't interrupt each other or struggle to see who would get the floor.

It is wonderful this inherent strength of weakness, as I might say, which enables a woman amid a throng of reckless men to command their respect and obedience sometimes where main strength and awkwardness would not avail.

(*Bill Nye and Boomerang*, 1881)

From *Answers to Correspondents*

The following answers to correspondents contain a great deal of useful information, and I publish them in order to avoid the constant annoyance of writing the same in substance to so many inquiring friends.

"Sweet Sixteen" writes from "Hold-up Hollow":

"I am betrothed to a noble youth from Rice Lake, Minnesota, but he seems to have soured on his betroth.

"At first he seemed to love me according to Gunter, but he has grown cold. About the first of the round-up he went away, and I soon afterward heard that he was affianced to another.

"I understand that he says I am not of noble lineage enough for him. It is true. I may not be a thoroughbred, but I have a pure, loving nature, which is now running to waste. The name of my beloved is De Courtney Van D'Edbeete. He comes from the first families, and O, I love him so!

"Can you tell me what to do?

"Sweet Sixteen."

Answer. Yes, I can tell you what to do. I have been there some, too. If you will only do as I tell you, you are safe.

You must win him back. I think you can easily do so.

Select a baseball club of about the weight you can handle easily, and then go to him and win him back.

You are too prone to give up easily. Do not be discouraged. All will yet be well.

He may think now that you are not of noble blood but you can make him change his mind. Go to him with the love light in your eye and put a triangular head on him with your baseball club, and tell him that he does not understand the cravings of your nature. Drive him into the ground and sit down on him, and then tell him that you are nothing but a poor, friendless girl, and need someone to cling to. Then you can cling to him. All depends upon how successful you are as a clinger.

I see at a glance that De Courtney needs to be flattened out a few times. Do not kill him, but bring him so near to the New Jerusalem that he can see the dome of the court house, and he will gradually come back to you and love you, and your life will be one long golden dream of never-fading joy, and De Courtney will wring out the colored clothes for you and help you do the washing, and he will stay at home evenings and take care of the children while you go to prayer meeting, and he will not murmur when you work off an inexpensive meal of cold rice and fricasseed codfish on him.

If he gets to feeling independent, and puts on the old air of defiance, you can diet him on cold mush and mackerel till he will not feel so robust, and then you can reason with him again, and while he is recovering you can take your baseball club and your noble self-sacrificing love, and win him back some more. . . .

(*Bill Nye and Boomerang*, 1881)

The Relentless Garden Hose

It is now the proper time for the cross-eyed woman to fool with the garden hose. I have faced death in almost every form and I do not know what fear is, but when a woman with one eye gazing into the zodiac and the other peering into the middle of next week and wearing one of those large floppy sunbonnets, picks up the nozzle of the garden hose and turns on the full force of the institution, I fly wildly to the Mountains of Hepsidam.

Water won't hurt anyone of course if care is used not to forget and drink any of it, but it is this horrible suspense and uncertainty about facing the nozzle of a garden hose in the hands of a cross-eyed woman that unnerves me and paralyzes me.

Instantaneous death is nothing to me. I am as cool and collected where leaden rain and iron hail are thickest, as I would be in my own office writing the obituary of the man who steals my jokes. But I hate to be drowned slowly in my good clothes and on dry land and have my dying gaze rest on a woman whose ravishing beauty would drive a narrow-gauge mule into convulsions and make him hate himself to death.

(*Bill Nye and Boomerang*, 1881)

A Fatal Thirst

From the London *Lancet* we learn that "many years ago a case was recorded by Dr. Otto, of Copenhagen, in which 495 needles passed through the skin of a hysterical girl, who had probably swallowed them during a hysterical paroxysm, but these all emerged from the regions below the diaphragm, and were collected in groups, which gave rise to inflammatory swellings of some size. One of these contained 100 needles. Quite recently Dr. Bigger described, before the Society Surgery, of Dublin, a case in which more than 300 needles were removed from the body of a woman. It is very remarkable in how few cases the needles were the cause of death, and how slight an interference with function their presence and movement cause."

It would seem from the cases on record that needles in the system rather assist in the digestion and promote longevity.

For instance, we will suppose that the hysterical girl above alluded to, with 495 needles in her stomach, should absorb the midsummer cucumber. Think how interesting those needles would make it for the great colic promoter.

We can imagine the cheerful smile of the cucumber as it enters the stomach, and bowing cheerfully to the follicles standing around, hangs its hat upon the walls of the stomach, stands its umbrella in a corner, and proceeds to get in its work.

All at once the cucumber looks surprised and grieved about something. It stops in its heaven-born colic generation and pulls a rusty needle out of its person. Maddened by the pain, it once more attacks the digestive apparatus, and once more accumulates a choice job lot of needles.

Again and again it enters into the unequal contest, each time losing ground and gaining ground, till the poor cucumber, with assorted hardware sticking out in all directions like the hair on a cat's tail, at last curls up like a caterpillar, and yields up the victory.

Still, this needle business will be expensive to husbands if wives once acquire the habit and allow it to obtain the mastery over them.

If a wife once permits this demon appetite for cambric needles to get control of the house, it will soon secure a majority in the senate, and then there will be trouble.

The woman who once begins to tamper with cambric needles is not safe. She may think that she has power to control her appetite, but it is only a step to the maddening thirst for the soul-destroying darning needle, and perhaps to the button-hook and carpet stretcher.

It is safer and better to crush the first desire for needles than when it is too late to undertake reformation from the abject slavery to this hellish thirst.

We once knew a sweet young creature with dewy eye and breath like timothy hay. Her merry laugh rippled out upon the summer air like the joyful music of baldheaded bobolinks.

Everybody loved her, and she loved everybody, too. But in a thoughtless moment she swallowed a cambric needle. This did not satisfy her. The cruel thraldom had begun. Whenever she felt depressed and gloomy there was nothing that would kill her ennui and melancholy but the fatal needle cushion.

From this she rapidly became more reckless, till there was hardly an hour that she was not under the influence of needles.

If she couldn't get needles to assuage her mad thirst, she would take hairpins or door keys. She gradually pined away to a mere skeleton. She could no longer sit on one foot and be happy.

Life for her was filled with opaque gloom and sadness. At last she took an overdose of sheep shears and monkey wrenches one day, and on the following morning her soul had lit out for the land of eternal summer.

We should learn from this to shun the maddening needle cushion as we would a viper, and never tell a lie.

(*Forty Liars, and Other Lies*, 1882)

The Female Barber

Women are now tackling every profession and style of business. There is hardly a path of life adown whose shaded paths we do not find the young lady sauntering in her charmingly careless manner.

Many of them are becoming barbers, and successful ones, too. There is a gentle touch required by a barber which is very grateful to the victim, and which is easily picked up by the lady apprentice.

There is a nameless joy steals into a man's soul when a musical voice tickles a man's ears as he lies in the chair with his eyes closed, while the tips of rosy fingers take him by the nose and pry open his mouth and a dainty twist of the wrist fills his back teeth full of soap and rain water.

O, woman! Little do you know what a power for good do you possess. When you jab a man's head back against the gable end of the barber chair, and hang it over behind so that his Adam's apple sticks up into the scented air like the breast bone of an old gobbler that has died of starvation, you have the great, manly lord of creation where he is as weak and tractable as a child.

Then you can wear him out with an old razor that you have shaved the whole broad universe with. Then you can peel off one feature after another and throw it into an old nail keg, and while you slice him up into sausage meat you can talk to him and make him think he is having a chunk of luxury ladled out to him such as no other living man ever got.

If a female barber is handsome, she can shave her customers with a bed-slat and powder their faces with Cayenne pepper and giant powder, and it will be all right.

A homely female barber, however, would have nothing to do but to hone up old razors and think about the sombre past.

(*Forty Liars, and Other Lies*, 1882)

Woman's Suffrage in Wyoming

The managing editor of a Boston paper is getting material together relative to the practical workings of woman's suffrage, and as Wyoming is at present working a scheme of that kind, he wants an answer to the following questions:

1. — Has it been of real benefit to the territory?
2. — If so, what has it accomplished?
3. — How does it affect education, morals, courts, etc.?
4. — What proportion of the women vote?

ANSWERS

1. — Yes, it has indeed been of real benefit to the territory in many ways. Until woman's suffrage came among us, life was a drag—a monotonous sameness, and simultaneous continuousness. Now it is not that way. Woman comes forward with her ballot, and puts new life into the flagging energies of the great political circles. She purifies the political atmosphere, and comes to the polls with her suffrage done up in a little wad, and rammed down into her glove, and redeems the country.

2. — It has accomplished more than the great outside world wots of. Philosophers and statesmen may think that they wot; but they don't. Not a wot.

To others outside of Wyoming, woman's suffrage is a mellow dream; but here it is a continuous, mellow, yielding reality. We know what we are talking about. We are acquainted with a lady who came here with the light of immortality shining in her eye, and the music of the spheres was singing in her ears. She was apparently on her last limbs, if we may be allowed that expression. But woman's suffrage came to her with healing on its wings, and the rose of health again bloomed on her cheek, and her appetite came back like the famine in Ireland. Now she wrestles with the cast-iron majolica ware of the kitchen during the day, and in the evening works a cross-eyed elephant on a burlap tidy, and talks about the remonetization of the currency.

Without attempting to answer the last two questions in a short article like this, we will simply give a few certificates and testimonials of those who have tried it:

Prairie-Dog Ranche, Jan. 3, 1888.

"*Dear Sir:* I take great pleasure in bearing testimony to the efficacy of woman's suffrage. It is indeed a boon to thousands. I was troubled in the East beyond measure with an ingrowing nail on the most extensive toe. It caused me great pain and annoyance. I was compelled to do my work wearing an old gum over-shoe of my husband's. Since using woman's suffrage only a few months, my toe is entirely well, and I now wear my husband's fine boots with perfect ease. As a remedy for ingrowing nails I can safely recommend the woman's suffrage.

Sassafras Oleson."

Miner's Delight, Jan. 23, 1888.

"*Deer Sur:* Two year ago mi waife fell down into a nold sellar and droav her varyloid through the Sarah bellum. I thot she was a Gonner. I woz then livin' in the sou west potion of Injeanny. I moved to where i now am leaving sevral onsettled accounts where i lived. But i wood do almost anything to recover mi waifs helth. She tried Woman's Suffrins and can now lick me with 1 hand tied behind hur.

i o everything to the free yuse of the femail ballot. So good bi

at Present Union Forever McGilligin."

Rawhide, Feb. 2, 1888.

"*Dear Sir:* I came to Wyoming one year ago today. At that time I only weighed 153 pounds and felt all the time as though I might die. I was a walking skeleton. Coyotes followed me when I went away from the house.

"My husband told me to try Woman's Suffrage. I did so. I have now run up to my old weight of 213 pounds, and I feel that with the proper care and rest, and rich wholesome diet, I may be spared to my husband and family till next spring.

"I am now joyful and happy. I go about my work all day singing Old Zip Coon and other plaintive melodies. After using Woman's Suffrage two days I sat up in a rocking chair and ate one and three-fourths mince pies. Then I worried down a sugar-cured ham and have been gaining ever since.

"Ah! it is a pleasant thing to come back to life and its joys again.

Yours truly,
Ethel Lillian Kersikes."

(*Bill Nye's Chestnuts, Old and New*, 1887)

"Oh, Wilhelmina, Come Back!"

PERSONAL — Will the young woman who edited the gravy department and corrected proof at our pie foundry for two days and then jumped the game on the evening that we were to have our clergyman to dine with us, please come back, or write to 32 Park Row, saying where she left the crackers and cheese?

Come back, Wilhelmina, and be our little sunbeam once more. Come back and cluster around our hearthstone at so much per cluster.

If you think best we will quit having company at the house, especially people who do not belong to your set.

We will also strive, oh so hard, to make it pleasanter for you in every way. If we had known four or five years ago that children were offensive to you, it would have been different. But it is too late now. All we can do is to shut them up in a barn and feed them through a knot-hole. If they shriek loud enough to give pain to your throbbing brow, let no one know and we will overcome any false sentiment we may feel towards them and send them to the Tombs.

Since you went away we can see how wicked and selfish we were and how little we considered your comfort. We miss your glad smile, also your Tennessee marble cake and your slat pie. We have learned a valuable lesson since you went away, and it is that the blame should not have rested on one alone. It should have been divided equally, leaving me to bear half of it and my wife the other half.

Where we erred was in dividing up the blame on the basis of tenderloin steak or peach cobbler, compelling you to bear half of it yourself. That will not work, Wilhelmina. Blame and preserves do not divide on the same basis. We are now in favor of what may be called a sliding scale. We think you will like this better.

We also made a grave mistake in the matter of nights out. While young, I formed the wicked and pernicious habit of having nights out myself. I panted for the night air and would go a long distance and stay out a long time to get enough of it for a mess and then bring it home in a paper bag, but I can see now that it is time for me to remain indoors and give young people like yourself a chance, Wilhelmina.

So, if I can do anything evenings while you are out that will assist you, such as stoning raisins or neighboring windows, command me. I am no cook, of course, but I can peel apples or grind coffee or hold your head for you when you need sympathy. I could also soon learn to do the plain cooking, I think, and friends who come to see us after this have agreed to bring their dinners.

There is no reason why harmony should not be restored among us and the old sunlight come back to our roof tree.

Another thing I wish to write before I close this humiliating personal. I wish to take back my harsh and bitter words about your singing. I said that you sang like a shingle-mill, but I was mad when I said it, and I wronged you. I was maddened by hunger and you told me that mush and milk was the proper thing for a brain worker, and you refused to give me any dope on my dumpling. Goaded to madness by this I said that you sang like a shingle-mill, but it was not my better, higher nature that spoke. It was my grosser and more gastric nature that asserted itself, and I now desire to take it back. You do not sing like a shingle-mill; at least so much as to mislead a practiced ear.

Your voice has more volume, and when your upper register is closed, is mellower than any shingle-mill I ever heard.

Come back, Wilhemina. We need you every hour.

After you went away we tried to set the bread as we had seen you do it, but it was not a success. The next day it came off the nest with a litter of small, sallow rolls which would easily resist the action of acids.

If you cannot come back will you please write and tell me how you are getting along and how you contrive to insert air-holes into home-made bread?

(*Nye and Riley's Railway Guide*, 1888)

CHAPTER 7

Partial Portraits

Fine-Cut as a Means of Grace

The amateur tobacco chewer many times through lack of consideration allows himself to be forced into very awkward and unpleasant positions. As a fair sample of the perils to which the young and inexperienced masticator of the weed is subjected, the following may be given:

A few Sabbaths ago a young man who was attending divine worship up on Piety Avenue, concluded, as the sermon was about one-half done and didn't seem to get very exciting, that he would take a chew of tobacco. He wasn't a handsome chewer, and while he was sliding the weed out of his pocket and getting it behind his handkerchief and working it into his mouth, he looked as though he might be robbing a blind woman of her last copper. Then when he got it into his mouth and tried to look pious and anxious about the welfare of his never dying soul, the chew in his mouth felt as big as a Magnolia ham. Being new in the business, the salivary glands were so surprised that they began to secrete at a remarkable rate. The young man got alarmed. He wanted to spit. His eyes began to hang out on his cheek, and still the salivary glands continued to give down. He thought about spitting in his handkerchief or his hat, but neither seemed to answer the purpose. He was getting wild. He thought of swallowing it, but he knew that his stomach wasn't large enough.

In his madness he resolved that he would let drive down the aisle when the pastor looked the other way. He waited till the divine threw his eyes toward heaven and then he shut his eyes and turned loose. An old gentleman about three pews down the aisle yawned at that moment and threw his open hand into the aisle in such a manner as to catch the contribution without any loss to speak of. He did not put his hand out for that purpose and did not seem to want it, but he got it all right.

He seemed to feel hurt about something. He looked like a man who has suddenly lost faith in humanity and become soured, as it were. Some who sat near him said he swore. Anyway, he lost the thread of the discourse. That part of the sermon he now says is a blank to him. It is several blanks. He called upon blank to everlastingly blank such a blankety blank blank, idiotic blank fool as the young man was.

Meantime the young man has quit the use of tobacco. He did not know at first whether to swear off or kill himself. The other day he said: "Only two weeks ago I stood up and said proudly I amateur. Today, praise be to redeeming grace, I am not a chewer." (This joke for the first few days will have to be watered very carefully and wrapped in a California blanket, for it is not strong at all. However, if it can be worked through the cold weather it is no slouch of a joke.)

(*Bill Nye and Boomerang*, 1881)

An Evidence of Spring

The imperial czar of all the tramps was in town to-day. He is traveling *in cog.*, and don't want us to say anything about his presence in the city, for fear the nihilists would get after him.

He is making his sixteenth grand semi-annual farewell bridal tour of the United States. He is a bachelor.

This tramp has the spring style of trousseau, consisting of a costume which, by pulling a tenpenny nail out of the bias folds in front, the entire costume will fall to pieces.

He is looking over the town with a view to investment. If the saloon keepers will leave enough beer in the kegs they stand out on the sidewalks to make a bonus sufficient to warrant him in remaining here, he will do so. He is highly pleased with the town, and says that people have been very kind to him so far, leaving their washings out on the line till after the gloaming, and in other ways showing their free, open, generous western natures.

He says Laramie seems to be a good summer resort for health and pleasure seekers, and that the chickens do not roost so high as he feared they would.

The imperial czar of all tramps says that the ovation tendered him by the police yesterday was very gratifying.

He says he would have made some remarks to that effect, but before he could recover his composure and get his spinal column back into plumb, the police had retired and were kicking a tramp over the top of the opera house by request.

The imperial czar wears his hair cut curly, with axle grease and hay in it. He is not very fastidious in his personal appearance, but dresses like a spring poet. He will, this afternoon, once more appear in his favorite flying leap through space, followed by the box-toed boot of the marshal.

(*Forty Liars, and Other Lies*, 1882)

They Let Him Stay

In the early history of Cummins City, when Calamity and Lengthy Johnson and Tapeworm Charlie were the bon ton of the new gold camp, there was a man whom we will call Doctor Farrar, who went there partially to assay for the camp, and partially to wear out his young life. Doctor Farrar had a pretty up-hill job of it from the start, for the mines hadn't boomed very fast at first, and a good many of the boys sent their samples of ore to Salt Lake or Denver for assay, and the rest of them used to salt his flax and get a big showing, and then stand him up for his pay. One honest miner gilded his pestle one night in the assay office, and sold his gopher-hole on Vinegar Hill the next day on an assay of $1,528 to the ton.

After awhile Doctor Farrar found that he had to lock up his mortar and flax in his trunk and sleep with his crucibles, or his reputation as an assayist would become a by-word and a stench in the nostrils of the pilgrim with the plug hat, and the tenderfoot would say, "*Fie* upon him," and spit upon him, and smite him on the bugle.

On top of all this an injurious report got out over the camp reflecting upon the morality of Doctor Farrar. Society was in a crude state, and most every stove-pipe in town had been bored so full of bullet holes that it wouldn't draw, and there was a general feeling of insecurity.

Most every one said that unless steps were taken to quiet things a little before long, there would be music by the entire band.

It was generally decided that the vigilanters would have to begin on Doctor Farrar. The town was getting a bad reputation outside, and something must be done. The committee, however, was not in working order, as a part of the number had gone over toward Last Chance on a placer stampede, and half a dozen more were in Laramie on district court business. However, it was decided that two members of the committee, whom we will call Trustworthy Kersikes and "The Annihilator" were delegated to arm themselves and drive Dr. Farrar out of town or inform him they would shoot him on sight.

Great care was used to prevent Dr. Farrar from getting any premature notice of this arrangement, because those who knew his very shrinking and gentle disposition were sure that if he were to drop on the programme he would skip the camp, and the amusement would have to be postponed.

It was therefore decided that Trustworthy Kersikes and "The Annihilator" should go down to the assay office armed and prepared to either scare the assayer to death or spatter his quivering flesh all over Pole Cat avenue.

About opposite the palatial dugout occupied by Calamity the avengers met Dr. Farrar.

He had just been down to Sam Wood's and hoisted in about six fingers of what was known at that time as Vinegar Hill Sheep Dip. It was waybilled over the Union Pacific as "Liquid Crime."

The avengers stood back a moment to give the fugitive a chance to escape if he wanted to, but he didn't avail himself of it.

He seemed to court death.

He simply walked up to Trustworthy Kersikes and twisted the double-barrel shotgun out of his hands like a flash. Then he pulled in on "The Annihilator" and told him to throw up his hands. Calmly as though he were making an assay on Gilt Edge blossom rock, Dr. Farrar went through the garments of the avengers. The six-shooters he stowed away in the bust of his pantaloons, and the double-barrel shotgun he broke over a pine log and threw it up on the woodshed.

Then he told the avengers that he would spare their unprofitable lives this trip, but if they ever tried to kill him again there would be a good deal of hilarity on the main street. He said he was not of a revengeful or antagonistic disposition, but that if this thing was repeated every evening with a matinee for ladies and children every Saturday afternoon, he would get a repeating hoe handle and clean out the entire vigilance committee.

Doctor Farrar said he had never been looked upon as a quarrelsome or deadly man at all; he was just a plain, everyday style of citizen, without any consuming ambition to fill the world with funerals, and hang a sable pall of mourning over the land; but if the vigilance committee wanted to make an example of him, and would give him notice enough so that he could arm himself with an old salt-bag full of convalescent eggs, and an old pick handle, he would be willing to abide the result.

The committee turned in silent scorn and left him, and the disagreeable subject was never broached afterward.

(*Forty Liars, and Other Lies*, 1882)

The Champion Mean Man

Laramie has the champion mean man. He has a Sunday handkerchief made to order with scarlet spots on it, which he sticks up to his nose just before the plate starts round, and leaves the church like a house on fire. So after he has squeezed out the usual amount of gospel, he slips around the corner and goes home ten cents ahead, and has his self-adjusting nose-bleed handkerchief for another trip.

(*Baled Hay*, 1884)

The Humorist Interviews His Grace in the Improved Style

Newport, Sept. 8.

I have just terminated a pleasant call upon the Duke of Marbro at his lodgings. I write his name Marbro because that is the way we pronounce it here at Newport. In the language of my ostensibly colored friend, Mr. Rankin, the amateur pronouncer would call it Marl-bor-ough, with three grunts, while in fact Marbro, the correct pronunciation of the name, is executed with but one grunt.

I found the Duke seated on a low ottoman, clad in a loosely fitting costume of pajamas. It was so loose and neglige that it was on the tip of my tongue to ask him if his mother made it for him out of his father's old pajamas; but I suddenly remembered that I was in Newport, and not in Tombstone, Arizona, and I restrained myself.

The Duke is suffering from a slight cold, which he contracted for during the early part of the week. It resulted from his ignorance of our changeable and freckle-minded climate. On Tuesday he took a long stroll, and while several miles from his lodgings and wearing his light summer cane, he was overtaken by a severe and sudden change in the temperature. The Marbros are not a strong race, and I am told that one of the Duke's second cousins died of pneumonia from exposing himself to the severity of a Christmas-day frolic clad in an autumn cane.

The Duke rose languidly as I entered, and, taking a reef in his pajamas clothes, looked at me in an inquiring way which betokened that, though of lineage high, he was not entirely at his ease in my presence.

"Duke," said I, standing my umbrella up in the corner to show my childlike confidence in him, "how's your conduct?"

In five minutes afterwards I would have given worlds if I could have recalled my rash words. I did not mean anything more than to utter a piece of pleasantry, for I am passionately fond of pleasantry even in society; but Marbro seemed to take it to heart and to feel distressed. He made a low, guttural sound, but his reply seemed to die away in the mansard roof of his mouth. He stammered out something which sounded like the wail of a damned soul. At least it struck me to be like that, although my lot has not been cast among that class of souls since I got out of politics, and I may have forgotten their style of wail.

To hide his embarrassment, Marbro "rosined" his eye and put a large glass paper weight in it. He then regarded me with some amazement through this piece of brick-a-brac, while I poured out a grown person's dose of Rectified Ruin which stood on the escritoire and drank it with a keen relish, which showed that I trusted him implicitly. Everything I did was done to make Marbro forget himself and feel at his ease.

I told him I had known the Marbros in Maine ever since I was a boy; that we didn't feel above them then, and it would be a poor time to begin now at my time of life to look down on people just because I now wrote pieces for the paper, many of which were afterwards printed. We always thought that the Marbros, or Marlboroughs, of Maine, got their name from burrowing in the marl along the Piscataquis, I said.

Thus I chatted on with him for an hour or two without seeming to chirk him up at all. "Duke," said I at last, "I know what the matter must be with you—you are socially ostracized. I knew it as soon as I came into the room. You cannot disguise it from me. You are suffering from social ostracism, and it is breaking you down. The social demands made by America upon an imported social wreck do not give said wreck time to eat his meals and obtain a necessary amount of rest. I suppose there is nowhere in the world a climate that is so trying on a person suffering from social ostracism as that of my native land. In other climes they give a social outcast rest, but here he gets absolutely no rest whatever."

I then drifted into society chat in a graceful and naïve way, which, with others, has never failed to melt the stoniest heart. I told him that I had understood, since I came to Newport, that the demands of society here were so unrelenting that they had kept Mr. and Mrs. Mayonnaise dressing all the time.

A long pause ensued here, during which I could hear Marbro's reason tottering on its throne. After waiting three-quarters of an hour, by my watch, and failing to see that my remark had shed even a ray of sunshine, where erstwhile all was gloom and chaos, I gave him my address and told him that if, in the future, he ever derived any beneficial effects from the above joke, I would be glad to have him communicate with me. And even if I were to die before he could truly say that he had been benefited by this joke and grapple with its keen, incisive nub, my grandchildren would be tickled almost to death to know that he had taken it to pieces and put it together again and found out how it was built and laugh at its ingenious mechanism.

I conversed with the Duke some time about the way his visit to Newport had depressed the price of real estate, and offered him the freedom of New York, hoping that he could depress the price of real estate there so that I could buy some.

"But," said I, assuming an air of perfect repose, as I flung myself on a low couch in such a way as to give a faint view of my new red socks, "you will find it different in New York. Social ostracism there will not materially affect the price of real estate in the neighborhood of the postoffice. In fact, Marbro," said I, regarding him earnestly for a moment through the bottom of a cut-glass tumbler, "there is not enough English social ostracism in New York to supply the demand. Come to our young and thriving town, a town that is rich in resources and liabilities; a town that threatens to rival Omaha as a railroad center; a town where a B. and O. deal has been a common occurrence every day for over a year; a town where you can ride on the elevated trains and get yourself pinched in the iron gate by the guard or go down to Wall street and get pinched by the directors; a town where a man like Henry S. Ives can buy about seven million dollars' worth of stuff that he can't pay for, while a poor man who goes into a general store to buy a pair of ear muffs is followed up by a private detective for fear he may run his finger into the molasses barrel and then lick it syruptitiously. "Come on, Duke," said I, growing more talkative as the fumes of his fifty-two dollar liquor rose to my surprised and delighted brains; "come on to New York and mix up with us, and get on to our ways.

"See Fulton market by midnight, bite off a piece of atmosphere from Castle Garden, and come with me to see Guiteau's head in the museum. Guiteau was the last of a long line of assassins. He prophesied that every one connected with his trial would come to a bad end. Quite a number of those connected with this celebrated trial are already dead, and more especially Mr. Guiteau himself, whose skeleton is in the Smithsonian Institution, his viscera in the Potomac, and his head in a jar of alcohol. If you will come to New York, Marbro, you will have a good time, and the rose geraniums will come back to your pallid and durable cheek.

"If you will give us a whirl, Duke," said I, selecting an umbrella from the decorated crock in the hall and coming back to where he still sat, "you will be pleased and gratified with us; and if you can spare time to come over and see me personally I would try to be as cordial and chatty as you have been with me. No man ever entertained me as you have, or sat and examined me through the bottom of an old microscope for two hours, to be forgotten again by me. Marbro, if you will come to New York, we will go and visit anybody's tomb that you may designate."

I then let myself out of the house with an adjustable pass-key and hastened away. Shortly after I got back to my own lodgings, sometimes called a $7\frac{1}{8}$ room, a lackey from the Duke, wearing a livery-colored livery, handed me a note from Marbro, in which he said he hoped that in case I used this interview for publication I would be careful to give his exact language.

In my poor, weak way, I think I have done so.

(*Bill Nye's Chestnuts, Old and New*, 1887)

Anecdotes of Jay Gould

Facial neuralgia is what is keeping Jay Gould back this summer and preventing him from making as much money as he would otherwise. With good health and his present methods of doing business Mr. Gould could in a few years be beyond the reach of want, but he is up so much nights with his face that he has to keep one gas-jet burning all the time. Besides he has cabled once to Dr. Brown-Sequard for a neuralgia pill that he thought would relieve the intense pain, and found after he had paid for the cablegram that every druggist in New York kept the Brown-Sequard pill in stock. But when a man is ill he does not care for expense, especially when he controls an Atlantic cable or two.

This neuralgia pill is about the size of a two-year-old colt and pure white. I have been compelled to take several of them myself while suffering from facial neuralgia; for neuralgia does not spare the good, the true or the beautiful. She comes along and nips the poor yeoman as well as the millionaire who sits in the lap of luxury. Millionaires who flatter themselves that they can evade neuralgia by going and sitting in the lap of luxury make a great mistake.

"And do you find that this large porcelain pill relieves you at all, Mr. Gould?" I asked him during one of these attacks, as he sat in his studio with his face tied up in hot bran.

"No, it does me no good whatever," said the man who

likes to take a lame railroad and put it on its feet by issuing more bonds. "It contains a little morphine, which dulls the pain, but there's nothing in the pill to cure the cause. My neuralgia comes from indigestion. My appetite is four sizes too large for a man of my height and every little while I overeat. I then get dangerously ill and stocks become greatly depressed in consequence. I am now in a position where, if I had a constitution that would stand the strain, I could get well off in a few years. But I am not strong enough. Every little change in the weather affects me. I see a red-headed girl on the street and immediately afterwards I see one of these big white pills."

"Are you sure, Mr. Gould?" I asked him with some solicitude, as I bent forward and inhaled the rich fragrance of the carnation in his button-hole, "that you have not taken cold in some way?"

"Possibly I have," he said, as he shrank back in a petulant way, I thought. "Last week I got my feet a little damp while playing the hose on some of my stocks, but I hardly think that was what caused the trouble. I am apt to overeat, as I said. I am especially fond of fruit, too. When I was a boy I had no trouble, because I always divided my fruit with another boy, of whom I was very fond. I would always divide my fruit into two equal parts, keeping one of these and eating the other myself. Many and many a time when this boy and I went out together and only had one wormy apple between us, I have divided it and given him the worm.

"As a boy, I was taught to believe that half is always better than the hole."

"And are you not afraid that this neuralgia after it has picnicked around among your features may fly to your vitals?"

"Possibly so," said Mr. Gould, snapping the hunting case of his massive silver watch with a loud report, "but I am guarding against this by keeping my pocketbook wrapped up all the time in an old red flannel shirt."

Here Mr. Gould arose and went out of the room for a

long time, and I could hear him pacing up and down outside, stopping now and then to peer through the keyhole to see if I had gone away. But in each instance he was gratified to find that I had not. Lest any one should imagine that I took advantage of his absence to peruse his private correspondence, I will say here that I did not do so, as his desk was securely locked.

Mr. Gould's habits are simple and he does not hold his cane by the middle when he walks. He wears plain clothes and his shirts and collars are both made of the same shade. He says he feels sorry for any one who has to wear a pink shirt with a blue collar. Some day he hopes to endow a home for young men who cannot afford to buy a shirt and a collar at the same store.

He owes much of his neuralgia to a lack of exercise. Mr. Gould never takes any exercise at all. His reason for this is that he sees no prospect for exercise to advance in value. He says he is willing to take anything else but exercise.

Up to within a very few years Jay Gould has always slept well at night, owing to regular hours for rising and retiring and his careful abstinence from tobacco and alcohol. Lately neuralgia has kept him awake a good deal at night, but prior to that he used to sleep as sweetly and peacefully as a weasel.

The story circulated some years ago to the effect that a professional burglar broke into Mr. Gould's room in the middle of the night and before he could call the police was robbed of his tools, is not true. People who have no higher aim in life than the peddling about of such improbable yarns would do well to ascertain the truth of these reports before giving them circulation.

The story that Mr. Gould once killed a steer and presented his hoofs to the poor with the remark that it would help to keep sole and body together, also turned out to have no foundation whatever in fact, but was set afloat by an English wag who was passionately fond of a bit of pleasantry, don't you know.

Thus it is that a man who has acquired a competence by

means of honest toil becomes the target for the barbed shaft of contumely.

Mr. Gould is said to be a good conversationalist, though he prefers to close his eyes and listen to others. Nothing pleases him better than to lure a man on and draw him out and encourage him to turn his mind wrong side out and empty it. He then richly repays this confidence by saying that if it doesn't rain any more we will have a long dry time. The man then goes away inflated with the idea that he has a pointer from Mr. Gould which will materially affect values. A great many men are playing croquet at the poor-house this summer who owe their prosperity to tips given them by Mr. Gould.

As a fair sample of the way a story about a great man grows and becomes distorted at the same time, one incident will be sufficient. Some years ago, it is said, Mr. Gould bought a general admission ticket to hear Sarah Bernhardt as Camille. Several gentlemen who were sitting near where he stood asked him why he did not take a seat. Instead of answering directly that he could not get one he replied that he did not care for a seat, as he wanted to be near the door when the building fell. Shortly after this he had more seats than he could use. I give this story simply to illustrate how such a thing may be distorted, for upon investigation it was found to have occurred at a Patti concert, and not at a Bernhardt exhibition at all.

Mr. Gould's career, with its attendant success, should teach us two things, at least. One is, that it always pays to do a kind act, for a great deal of his large fortune has been amassed by assisting men like Mr. Field, when they were in a tight place, and taking their depressed stock off their hands while in a shrunken condition. He believes also that the merciful man is merciful to his stock.

He says he owes much of his success in life to economy and neuralgia. He also loves to relieve distress on Wall Street, and is so passionately fond of this as he grows older that he has been known to distress other stock men just for the pleasant thrill it gave him to relieve them.

Jay Gould is also a living illustration of what a young man may do with nothing but his bare hands in America. John L. Sullivan and Gould are both that way. Mr. Gould and Col. Sullivan could go into Siberia tomorrow—little as they are known there—and with a small Gordon press, a quire of bond paper and a pair of three-pennyweight gloves they would soon own Siberia, with a right of way across the rest of Europe and a first mortgage on the Russian throne. As fast as Col. Sullivan knocked out a dynasty Jay could come in and administer on the estate. This would be a powerful combination. It would afford us an opportunity also to get some of those Russian hay-fever names and chilblains by red message. Mr. Gould would get a good deal of money out of the transaction and Sullivan would get ozone.

(*Nye and Riley's Railway Guide*, 1888)

Roger Williams

. . . Roger Williams now settled at Providence Plantation, where he was joined by Mrs. Hutchinson, who also believed that the church and state should not be united, but that the state should protect the church and that neither should undertake to boss the other. It was also held that religious qualifications should not be required of political aspirants, also that no man should be required to whittle his soul into a shape to fit the religious auger-hole of another.

This was the beginning of Rhode Island. She desired at once to join the New England Colony, but was refused, as she had no charter. Plymouth claimed also to have jurisdiction over Rhode Island. This was very much like Plymouth.

Having banished Roger Williams and Mrs. Hutchinson to be skinned by the Pequods and Narragansetts over at Narragansett Pier, they went on about their business, flogging

Quakers, also ducking old women who had lumbago, and burning other women who would not answer affirmatively when asked, "Be you a witch?"

Then when Roger began to make improvements and draw the attention of Eastern capital to Rhode Island and to organize a State or Colony with a charter, Plymouth said, "Hold on, Roger: religiously we have cast you out, to live on wild strawberries, clams, and Indians, but from a mercantile and political point of view you will please notice that we have a string which you will notice is attached to your wages and discoveries."

Afterwards, however, Roger Williams obtained the necessary funds from admiring friends with which to go to England and obtain a charter which united the Colonies yet gave to all the first official right to liberty of conscience ever granted in Europe or America. Prior to that a man's conscience had a brass collar on it with the royal arms engraved thereon, and was kept picketed out in the king's grounds. The owner could go and look at it on Sundays, but he never had the use of it.

With the advent of freedom of political opinion, the individual use of the conscience has become popularized, and the time is coming when it will grow to a great size under our wise institutions and fostering skies. Instead of turning over our consciences to the safety deposit company of a great political party or religious organization and taking the key in our pocket, let us have individual charge of this useful little instrument and be able finally to answer for its growth or decay.

(*Bill Nye's History of the United States*, 1894)

The Dutch at New Amsterdam

Soon after the discovery of the Hudson, Dutch ships began to visit that region to traffic in furs with the Indians. Some huts were erected by these traders on Manhattan Island in 1613, and a trading-post was established in 1615. Relics of these times are frequently turned up yet on Broadway while putting in new pipes, or taking out old pipes, or repairing other pipes, or laying plans for yet other pipes, or looking in the earth to see that the original pipes have not been taken away.

Afterwards the West India Company obtained a grant of New Netherland, and New Amsterdam was fairly started. In 1626, Minuit, the first governor, arrived, and, as we have stated, purchased the entire city of New York of the Indians for twenty-four dollars.

Then trouble sprang up between the Dutch and the Swedes on the Delaware over the possession of Manhattan, and when the two tribes got to conversing with each other over their rights, using the mother-tongue on both sides, it reminded one of the Chicago wheat market when business is good. The English on the Connecticut also saw that Manhattan was going to boom as soon as the Indians could be got farther west, and that property would be high there.

Peter Stuyvesant was the last Dutch governor of New York. He was a relative of mine. He disliked the English very much. They annoyed him with their democratic ideas and made his life a perfect hell to him. He would be sorry to see the way our folks have since begun to imitate the English. I can almost see him rising in his grave to note how the Stuyvesants in full cry pursue the affrighted aniseseed bag, or with their coaching outfits go tooling along 'cross country, stopping at the inns on the way and unlimbering their portable bath-tubs to check them with the "clark."

Pete, you did well to die early. You would not have been happy here now.

While Governor Stuyvesant was in hot water with the English, the Swedes, and the Indians, a fleet anchored in the harbor and demanded the surrender of the place in the name of the Duke of York, who wished to use it for a game preserve. After a hot fight with his council, some of whom were willing even then to submit to English rule and hoped that the fleet might have two or three suits of tweed which by mistake were a fit and therefore useless to the owners, and that they might succeed in swapping furs for these, the governor yielded, and in 1664 New York became a British possession, named as above.

The English governors, however, were not popular. They were mostly political hacks who were pests at home and banished to New York, where the noise of the streets soon drove them to drink. For nine years this sort of thing went on, until one day a Dutch fleet anchored near the Staten Island brewery and in the evening took the town.

However, in the year following, peace was restored between England and Holland, and New Amsterdam became New York again, also subject to the Tammany rule.

Andros was governor for a time, but was a sort of pompous tomtit, with a short breath and a large aquiline opinion of himself. He was one of the arrogant old pieplants whose growth was fostered by the beetle-bellied administration at home. He went back on board the City of Rome one day, and did not return.

New York had a gleam of hope for civil freedom under the rule of the Duke of York and the county Democracy, but when the duke became James II. he was just like other people who get a raise of salary, and refused to be privately entertained by the self-made ancestry of the American.

He was proud and arrogant to a degree. He forbade legislation, and stopped his paper. New York was at this time annexed to the New England Colony, and began keeping the Sabbath so vigorously that the angels had great difficulty in getting at it.

Nicholson, who was the lieutenant tool of iniquity for Andros, fled with him when democracy got too hot for them. Captain Leisler, supported by Steve Brodie and everything south of the Harlem, but bitterly opposed by the aristocracy, who were distinguished by their ability to use new goods in making their children's clothes, whereas the democracy had to make vests for the boys from the cast-off trousers of their fathers, governed the province until Governor Sloughter arrived.

Sloughter was another imported Smearkase in official life, and arrested Leisler at the request of an aristocrat who drove a pair of bang-tail horses up and down Nassau Street on pleasant afternoons and was afterwards collector of the port. Having arrested Leisler for treason, the governor was a little timid about executing him, for he had never really killed a man in his life, and he hated the sight of blood; so Leisler's enemies got the governor to take dinner with them, and mixed his rum, so that when he got ready to speak, his remarks were somewhat heterogeneous, and before he went home he had signed a warrant for Leisler's immediate execution.

When he awoke in the morning at his beautiful home on Whitehall Street, the sun was gayly glinting the choppy waves of Buttermilk Channel, and by his watch, which had run down, he saw that it was one o'clock, but whether it was one o'clock a.m. or p.m. he did not know, nor whether it was next Saturday or Tuesday before last. Oh, how he must have felt!

His room was dark, the gas having gone out to get better air. He attempted to rise, but a chill, a throb, a groan, and back he lay hastily on the bed just as it was on the point of escaping him. Suddenly a thought came to him. It was not a great thought, but it was such a thought as comes to those who have been thoughtless. He called for a blackamoor slave from abroad who did chores for him, and ordered a bottle of cooking brandy, then some club soda he had brought from London with him. Next he drank a celery-glass of it, and after that he felt better. He then drank another.

"Keep out of the way of this bed, Julius," he said. "It is coming around that way again. Step to one side, Julius, please, and let the bed walk around and stretch its legs. I never saw a bed spread itself so," he continued, seeming to enjoy his own Lancashire humor. "All night I seemed to feel a great pain creeping over me, Julius," he said, hesitatingly, again filling his celery-glass, "but I see now that it was a counterpane."

Eighty years after that, Sloughter was a corpse.

We should learn from this not to be too hasty in selecting our birthplaces. Had he been born in America, he might have been alive yet.

From this on the struggles of the people up to the time of the Revolution were enough to mortify the reader almost to death. I will not go over them again. It was the history of all the other Colonies; poor, proud, with large masses of children clustering about, and Indians lurking in the out-buildings. The mother-country was negligent, and even cruel. Her political offscourings were sent to rule the people. The cranberry-crops soured on the vines, and times were very scarce.

It was during this period that Captain William Kidd, a New York shipmaster and anti-snapper from Mulberry Street, was sent out to overtake and punish a few of the innumerable pirates who then infested the high seas.

Studying first the character, life, and public services of the immoral pirate, and being perfectly foot-loose, his wife having eloped with her family physician, he determined to take a little whirl at the business himself, hoping thereby to escape the noise and heat of New York and obtain a livelihood while life lasted which would maintain him the remainder of his days unless death overtook him.

Dropping off at Boston one day to secure a supply of tobacco, he was captured while watching the vast number of street-cars on Washington Street. He was taken to England, where he was tried and ultimately hanged. His sudden and sickening death did much to discourage an American youth of great brilliancy who had up to 1868 intended to be a pirate, but who, stumbling across the "Life and Times of Captain Kidd, and his Awful Death," changed his whole course and became one of the ablest historians of the age in which he lived.

This should teach us to read the papers instead of loaning them to people who do not subscribe.

(*Bill Nye's History of the United States,* 1894)

The Battle of Quebec

. . . In 1759 General Wolfe anchored off Quebec with his fleet and sent a boy uptown to ask if there were any letters for him at the post-office, also asking at what time it would be convenient to evacuate the place. The reply came back from General Montcalm, an able French general, that there was no mail for the general, but if Wolfe was dissatisfied with the report he might run up personally and look over the W's.

Wolfe did so, taking his troops up by an unknown cowpath on the off side of the mountain during the night, and at daylight stood in battle-array on the Plains of Abraham. An attack was made by Montcalm as soon as he got over his wonder and surprise. At the third fire Wolfe was fatally wounded, and as he was carried back to the rear he heard some one exclaim,—

"They run! They run!"

"Who run?" inquired Wolfe.

"The French! The French!" came the reply.

"Now God be praised," said Wolfe, "I die happy."

Montcalm had a similar experience. He was fatally wounded. "They run! They run!" he heard some one say.

"Who run?" exclaimed Montcalm, wetting his lips with a lemonade-glass of cognac.

"We do," replied the man.

"Then so much the better," said Montcalm, as his eye lighted up, "for I shall not live to see Quebec surrendered."

This shows what can be done without a rehearsal; also how the historian has to control himself in order to avoid lying.

The death of these two brave men is a beautiful and dramatic incident in the history of our country, and should be remembered by every school-boy, because neither lived to write articles criticizing the other. . . .

(*Bill Nye's History of the United States*, 1894)

Noah Webster

. . . No American, foreign or domestic, ever made a greater name for himself than Daniel Webster, but he was not so good a penman as Noah; Noah was the better pen-writer.

Noah Webster also had the better command of language of the two. Those who have read his great work entitled "Webster's Elementary Spelling-Book, or, How One Word Led to Another," will agree with me that he was smart. Noah never lacked for a word by which to express himself. He was a brainy man and a good speller.

One by one our eminent men are passing away. Mr. Webster has passed away; Napoleon Bonaparte is no more; and Dr. Mary Walker is fading away. This has been a severe winter on Red Shirt; and I have to guard against the night air a good deal myself.

It would ill become me, at this late date, to criticise Mr. Webster's work, a work that is now, I may say, in nearly every home and schoolroom in the land. It is a great book. I only hope that had Mr. Webster lived he would have been equally fair in his criticism of my books.

I hate to compare my books with Mr. Webster's, because it looks egotistical in me; but, although Noah's book is larger than mine, and has more literary attractions as a book to set a child on at the table, it does not hold the interest of the reader all the way through.

He has introduced too many characters into his book at the expense of the plot. It is a good book to pick up and while away a leisure hour perhaps, but it is not a work that could rivet your interest till midnight, while the fire went out and the thermometer stepped down to 47° below zero. You do not hurry through the pages to see whether Reginald married the girl or not. Mr. Webster did not seem to care how the affair turned out.

Therein consists the great difference between Noah and myself. He doesn't keep up the interest. A friend of mine at Sing Sing, who secured one of my books, said he never left his room till he had devoured it. He said he seemed chained to the spot; and if you can't believe a convict who is entirely out of politics, whom, in the name of George Washington, can you trust?

Mr. Webster was certainly a most brilliant writer, though a little inclined, perhaps, to be wordy. I have discovered in some of his later books one hundred and eighteen thousand words no two of which are alike. This shows great fluency and versatility, it is true, but we need something else. The reader waits in vain to be thrilled by the author's wonderful word-painting. There is not a thrill in the whole tome.

I had heard so much of Mr. Webster that when I read his book I confess I was disappointed. It is cold, methodical, dry, and dispassionate in the extreme, and one cannot help comparing it with the works of James Fenimore Cooper and Horace.

As I said, however, it is a good book to pick up for the purpose of whiling away an idle hour. No one should travel without Mr. Webster's tale. Those who examine this tale will readily see why there were no flies on the author. He kept them off with this tale.

It is a good book, as I say, to take up for a moment, or to read on the train, or to hold the door open on a hot day. I would never take a long railroad ride without it, eyether. I would as soon forget my bottle of cough-medicine.

Mr. Webster's Speller had an immense sale. Ten years ago he had sold forty million copies. And yet it had this same defect. It was cold, dull, disconnected, and verbose. There was only one good thing in the book, and that was a little literary gem regarding a boy who broke in and stole the apples of a total stranger. The story was so good that I have often wondered whom Mr. Webster got to write it for him.

The old man, it seems, at first told the boy that he had better come down, as there was a draught in the tree; but the young sass-box—apple-sass-box, I presume—told him to avaunt.

At last the old man said, "Come down, honey. I am afraid the limb will break if you don't." Then, as the boy still remained, he told him that those were not eating-apples, that they were just common cooking-apples, and that there were worms in them. But the boy said he didn't mind a little thing like that. So then the old gentleman got irritated, and called the dog, and threw turf at the boy, and at last saluted him with pieces of turf and decayed cabbages; and after the lad had gone away the old man pried the bull-dog's jaws open and found a mouthful of pantaloons and a freckle.

I do not tell this, of course, in Mr. Webster's language, but I give the main points as they recur now to my mind.

Though I have been a close student of Mr. Webster for years and have carefully examined his style, I am free to say that his ideas about writing a book are not the same as mine. Of course it is a great temptation for a young author to write a book that will have a large sale; but that should not be all. We should have a higher object than that, and strive to interest those who read the book. It should not be jerky and scattering in its statements.

I do not wish to do an injustice to a great man who is now no more, a man who did so much for the world and who could spell the longest word without hesitation, but I speak of these things just as I would expect others to criticize my work. If one aspire to be a member of the *literati* of his day, he must expect to be criticized. I have been criticized myself. When I was in public life,—as a justice of the peace in the Rocky Mountains,—a man came in one day and criticized me so that I did not get over it for two weeks.

I might add, though I dislike to speak of it now, that Mr. Webster was at one time a member of the Legislature of Massachusetts. I believe that was the only time he ever stepped aside from the strait and narrow way. A good many people do not know this, but it is true.

Mr. Webster was also a married man, yet he never murmured or repined.

(*Bill Nye's History of the United States*, 1894)

Biography of Richard III

Being an Allegorical Panegyric of the Incontrovertible Machinations of an Egotistical Usurper

We will now write out a few personal recollections of Richard III. This great monarch, of whom so much has been said pro and con,—but mostly con,—was born at Fotheringhay Castle, October 2, 1452, in the presence of his parents and a physician whose name has at this moment escaped the treacherous memory of the historian.

Richard was the son of Richard, Duke of York, and Cecily Neville, daughter of the Earl of Westmoreland, his father being the legitimate heir to the throne by descent in the female line, so he was the head of the Yorkists in the War of the Roses.

Richard's father, the Duke of York, while struggling one day with Henry VI., the royal jackass that flourished in 1460, prior to the conquest of the Fool-Killer, had the misfortune, while trying to wrest the throne from Henry, to get himself amputated at the second joint. He was brought home in two pieces, and ceased to draw a salary as a duke from that on. This cast a gloom over Richard, and inspired in his breast a strong desire to cut off the heads of a few casual acquaintances.

He was but eight years of age at this time, and was taken prisoner and sent to Utrecht, Holland. He was returned in good order the following year. His elder brother Edward having become king, under the title of Edward IV., Richard was then made Duke of Gloucester, Lord High Admiral, Knight of the Garter, and Earl of Balmoral.

It was at this time that he made the celebrated *bon-mot* relative to dogs as pets.

Having been out the evening before attending a watermelon recital in the country, and having contributed a portion of his clothing to a barbed-wire fence and the balance to an open-faced Waterbury bull-dog, some one asked him what he thought of the dog as a pet.

Richard drew himself up to his full height, and said that, as a rule, he favored the dog as a pet, but that the man who got too intimate with the common low-browed bull-dog of the fifteenth century would find that it must certainly hurt him in the end.

He resided for several years under the tutelage of the Earl of Warwick, who was called the "King-maker," and afterwards, in 1470, fled to Flanders, remaining fled for some time. He commanded the van of the Yorkist army at the battle of Barnet, April 14, 1471, and Tewkesbury, May 4, fighting gallantly at both places on both sides, it is said, and admitting it in an article which he wrote for an English magazine.

He has been accused of having murdered Prince Albert

after the battle, and also his father, Henry VI., in the Tower a few days later, but it is not known to be a fact.

Richard was attainted and outlawed by Parliament at one time; but he was careful about what he ate, and didn't get his feet wet, so, at last, having a good preamble and constitution, he pulled through.

He married his own cousin, Anne Neville, who made a first-rate queen. She got so that it was no trouble at all for her to reign while Dick was away attending to his large slaughtering interests.

Richard at this time was made Lord High Constable and Keeper of the Pound. He was also Justiciary of North Wales, Seneschal of the Duchy of Lancaster, and Chief of Police on the North Side.

His brother Clarence was successfully executed for treason in February, 1478, and Richard, without a moment's hesitation, came to the front and inherited the estates.

Richard had a stormy time of it up to 1481, when he was made "protector and defender of the realm" early in May. He then proceeded with a few neglected executions. This list was headed—or rather beheaded—by Lord Chamberlain Hastings, who tendered his resignation in a pail of saw-dust soon after Richard became "protector and defender of the realm." Richard laid claim to the throne in June, on the grounds of the illegitimacy of his nephews, and was crowned July 6. So was his queen. They sat on this throne for some time, and each had a sceptre with which to welt their subjects over the head and keep off the flies in summer. Richard could wield a sceptre longer and harder, it is said, than any other middle-weight monarch known to history. The throne used by Richard is still in existence, and has an aperture in it containing some very old gin.

The reason this gin was left, it is said, was that he was suddenly called away from the throne and never lived to get back. No monarch should ever leave his throne in too much of a hurry.

Richard made himself very unpopular in 1485 by his

forced loans, as they were called: a system of assessing a man after dark with a self-cocking writ and what was known as the headache-stick, a small weapon which was worn up the sleeve during the day, and which was worn behind the ear by the loyal subject after nightfall. It was a common sight, so says the historian, to hear the nightfall and the headache-stick fall at the same time.

The queen died in 1485, and Richard thought some of marrying again; but it got into the newspapers because he thought of it while a correspondent was going by, who heard it and telegraphed his paper who the lady was and all about it. This scared Richard out, and he changed his mind about marrying, concluding, as a mild substitute, to go into battle at Bosworth and get killed all at once. He did so on the 22d of August.

After his death it was found that he had rolled up his pantaloons above his knees, so that he would not get gore on them. This custom was afterwards generally adopted in England.

He was buried by the nuns of Leicester in their chapel, Richmond then succeeding him as king. He was buried in the usual manner, and a large amount of obloquy heaped on him.

That is one advantage of being great. After one's grave is filled up, one can have a large three-cornered chunk of obloquy put on the top of it to mark the spot and keep medical students away of nights.

Greatness certainly has its drawbacks, as the Duchess of Bloomer once said to the author, after she had been sitting on a dry-goods box with a nail in it, and had, therefore, called forth adverse criticism. An unknown man might have sat on that same dry-goods box and hung on the same nail till he was black in the face without causing remarks, but with the Duchess of Bloomer it was different,—oh, so different!

(Bill Nye's *History of England from the Druids to the Reign of Henry VIII*, 1896)

CHAPTER *8*

The Human Condition

The Modern Parlor Stove

In view of the new and apparently complex improvements in heating stoves, and the difficulty of readily operating them successfully, a word or two as to their correct management may not be out of place at this time.

Some time since, having worn out my old stove and thrown it aside, I purchased a new one called the "Fearfully and Wonderfully Maid." It had been highly spoken of by a friend, so I set it up in the parlor, turned on steam, threw the throttle wide open, and waited to see how it would operate. At the first stroke of the piston I saw that something was wrong with the reversible turbine wheel, and I heard a kind of grating sound, no doubt caused by the rubbing of the northeast trunnion on the face plate of the ratchet-slide. Being utterly ignorant of the workings of the stove, I attempted to remedy this trouble without first reversing the boomerang, and in a few moments the gas accumulated so rapidly that the cross-head gave way, and the right ventricle of the buffer-beam was blown higher than Gilroy's kite, carrying with it the saddle-plate, bull-wheel and monkey-wrench. Of course it was very careless to overlook what the merest schoolboy ought to know, for not only were all these parts of the stove a total wreck, but the crank-arbor, walking-beam and throat-latch were twisted out of shape, and so mixed up with the feed-cam, tumbling-rod, thumb-screw, dial-plate and colic indicator, that I was obliged to send for a practical engineer at an expense of $150, with board and travelling expenses, to come and fix it up.

Now, there is nothing more simple than the operation of one of these stoves, with the most ordinary common sense. At first, before starting your fire, see that the oblique diaphragm and eccentric shaft are in their true position; then step to the rear of the stove and reverse the guide plate, say three-quarters of an inch, force the stretcher bar forward and loosen the gang-plank. After this, start your fire, throw open the lemon-squeezer and right oblique hydraulic, see that the tape-worm pinion and Aurora Borealis are well oiled, bring the rotary pitman forward until it corresponds with the maintop mizzen, let go the smoke stack, horizontal duodenum, thorough brace and breech-pin, and as the stove begins to get under way you can slide forward the camera; see that the ramrod is in its place, unscrew the cerebellum, allow the water gauge to run up to about 75° in the shade, keep your eye on the usufruct, and the stove cannot fail to give satisfaction. The Fearfully and Wonderfully Maid may not be a cheap or durable stove, but for simplicity and beauty of execution, she seems to excel and lay over, and everlastingly get away with all other stoves, by a very large majority.

(*Bill Nye and Boomerang*, 1881)

A Tearful Appeal

There is a good deal of interest manifested these days on the part of the American people relative to the matter of separate sleeping cars for the two sexes. It is a move in the right direction, and we hope it will win. As it is now, no gentleman traveling alone is safe.

Several months ago, entirely alone, we traveled from Laramie to Chicago and back, making the round trip with no escort whatever. Our wife was detained at home, and that entire journey was made with no one to whom we could look for protection.

When we returned our hair had turned perfectly white with the horror of those dreadful nights.

There was one woman from Philadelphia, whose name we will not mention, and who rode all the way between Omaha and Chicago in our car. Almost the first thing when we started out of Omaha, she began to make advances toward us by asking us if we would not hold her lunch basket while she went after a drink.

She also asked us for our knife to peel an orange.

These things look small and insignificant, but in the light of later developments they are of vital importance.

That evening we saw with horror that the woman's section was adjoining our own!

We asked the conductor if this could not be changed, but he laughed coldly, and told us to soak our head, or some such unfeeling remark.

That is one bad feature of the present system. A man traveling alone gets no sympathy or assistance from the conductor.

It would be impossible to describe the horror and apprehension of that awful night. All through its vigils we suffered on till near morning, when tired nature yielded, and we fell into a troubled sleep.

There we lay, fair and beautiful, in the soft gray of approaching day, thousands of miles from our home, and, less than feet away, a great, horrid woman from Pennsylvania, to whom we had not even been introduced.

How we could sleep so soundly, under the circumstances, we are yet unable to tell, but after perhaps twenty minutes of slumber, we saw, above the footboard of our berth and peering over at us, the face of that woman. With a wild bound we were on our feet in the aisle of the car. The other berths had all disappeared but ours.

The other passengers were sitting quietly in their seats, and it was half-past 9 o'clock. The woman from Pennsylvania was in the day coach.

It was only a horrid dream.

But supposing that it had been a reality! Any man who travels alone is liable to be insulted at any time. We do not care for luxury in traveling. All we want is the assurance that we are safe.

The experience which we have narrated above is only one of a thousand. Did you ever note the careworn look of the man who is traveling alone? The wild, hunted expression on the countenance and the horrible apprehension that is depicted there?

You may talk about the various causes that are leading men downward to early graves, but the nervous strain induced by the fear that while they are taking out their false teeth or buttoning their suspenders, prying eyes are looking over the footboard of their berths, is constructing more new-made graves than consumption or the Ute war.

(*Forty Liars, and Other Lies*, 1882)

Growing Old

What can be sadder than to feel the chill autumn of life coming on when the shady side of the valley has been reached and the eye is turned backward toward the green and sunlit fields which exist in memory alone. How sadly settles down upon the human heart the sorrowful truth that the brightest and best of existence has fled. The tear will unbidden start as we think of those years replete with gladness now gone forever. Those dear, delightful years before we trod the rough and rugged road of experience and bit off more than we could masticate. One by one we count the priceless bits of knowledge we have gained and look over the store as the miser reckons his treasure.

We call to mind how the cold, clammy truth was revealed to us at one time that, in gathering the full-blown roses of life, too oft we gather also the feverish and irritable bumble bee nestling in its petals.

How freshly now comes back to us the memory of that bright autumnal day when the sky was one vast sea of golden billows and the spicy aroma of decaying vegetation pervaded everything; that day when we made some scientific experiments with what is called three card monte and went home without our overcoat.

This was a long time ago, but how fresh it is in our memory, and how fresh it seemed to our parents when we unfolded the account of our scientific experiments.

Yes, we are not so frolicsome now as we were forty or fifty years ago, but we know more. It is true we cannot go in swimming all day with impunity or walk around a billiard table all day and then glide through the Blue Danube waltz all night as we once could, but we have acquired some high-priced experience and put it where we can get at it.

We were making an estimate last evening of the value of a few items of experience which we now have on hand, and among the more valuable ones we will name the following:

Cost of experiments with mixed drinks, $2,000.

Expense of calling a large, healthy man a liar, $50.

Experiments in going without underclothes, $5,750.

Experiments with ostensibly disabled hornets, $375.

Cost of winning the love and confidence of an orphan mule, $500.

Little lessons in investigating different games of chance, with a view to making them a business, $2,500.

Experiments with watermelons, guarded by irritable bulldogs, $525.

Cost of unavailing efforts to prevent baldness, $783.20

Expense of personal investigation of lotteries, $935.26.

Actual cost of obtaining $13 worth of fame, which is

now for sale at the above price and still in good working order, though slightly tarnished, $17,380.

There are other expensive little nuggets and gobs of ripe experience that we have on hand, and we cannot look on them without a pardonable pride.

'Tis true that what we have learned is not very valuable to others, but it is a good thing to have, and we can use it right along in our business. We will try to work it off on our oldest son when he gets here, but he will not use it.

He would rather go and buy it the way we did. Information that don't cost $2,000 a hunk is no good. It comes high, but we must have it.

(*Forty Liars, and Other Lies*, 1882)

Fraternal Sparring

I have just returned from a little two-handed tournament with the gloves. I have filled my nose with cotton waste so that I shall not soak this sketch in gore as I write.

I needed a little healthful exercise and was looking for something that would be full of vigorous enthusiasm, and at the same time promote the healthful flow of blood to the muscles. This was rather difficult. I tried most everything, but failed. Being a sociable being (joke) I wanted other people to help me exercise, or go along with me when I exercised. Some men can go away to a desert isle and have fun with dumb-bells and a horizontal bar, but to me it would seem dull and commonplace after a while, and I would yearn for more humanity.

Two of us finally concluded to play billiards; but we were only amateurs and the owner intimated that he would want the table for Fourth of July, so we broke off in the middle of the first game and I paid for it.

Then a younger brother said he had a set of boxing-gloves in his room, and although I was the taller and had longer arms, he would hold up as long as he could, and I might hammer him until I gained strength and finally got well.

I accepted this offer because I had often regretted that I had not made myself familiar with this art, and also because I knew it would create a thrill of interest and fire me with ambition, and that's what a hollow-eyed invalid needs to put him on the road to recovery.

The boxing-glove is a large fat mitten, with an abnormal thumb and a string at the wrist by which you tie it on, so that when you feed it to your adversary he cannot swallow it and choke himself. I had never seen any boxing-gloves before, but my brother said they were soft and wouldn't hurt anybody. So we took off some of our raiment and put them on. Then we shook hands. I can remember distinctly yet that we shook hands. That was to show that we were friendly and would not slay each other.

My brother is a great deal younger than I am and so I warned him not to get excited and come for me with anything that would look like wild and ungovernable fury, because I might, in the heat of debate, pile his jaw up on his forehead and fill his ear full of sore thumb. He said that was all right and he would try to be cool and collected.

Then we put our right toes together and I told him to be on his guard. At that moment I dealt him a terrific blow aimed at his nose, but through a clerical error of mine it went over his shoulder and spent itself in the wall of the room, shattering a small holly-wood bracket, for which I paid him $3.75 afterward. I did not wish to buy the bracket because I had two at home, but he was arbitrary about it and I bought it.

We then took another athletic posture, and in two seconds the air was full of poulticed thumb and buckskin mitten. I soon detected a chance to put one in where my brother could smell of it, but I never knew just where it struck, for at that moment I ran up against something with the pit of my stomach that made me throw up the sponge along with some other groceries, the names of which I cannot now recall.

My brother then proposed that we take off the gloves, but I thought I had not sufficiently punished him, and that another round would complete the conquest, which was then almost within my grasp. I took a bismuth powder and squared myself, but in warding off a left-hander, I forgot about my adversary's right and ran my nose into the middle of his boxing-glove. Fearing that I had injured him, I retreated rapidly on my elbows and shoulder-blades to the corner of the room, thus giving him ample time to recover. By this means my younger brother's features were saved, and are to-day as symmetrical as my own.

I can still cough up pieces of boxing-gloves, and when I close my eyes I can see calcium lights and blue phosphorescent gleams across the horizon; but I am thoroughly convinced that there is no physical exercise which yields the same amount of health and elastic vigor to the puncher that the manly art does. To the punchee, also, it affords a large wad of glad surprises and nose bleed, which cannot be hurtful to those who hanker for the pleasing nervous shock, the spinal jar and the pyrotechnic concussion.

That is why I shall continue the exercises after I have practiced with a mule or a cow-catcher two or three weeks, and feel a little more confidence in myself.

(*Baled Hay*, 1884)

Preserving Eggs

The Scientific American gives this as an excellent mode of preserving eggs: "Take fresh ones, put a dozen or more into a small willow basket, and immerse this for five seconds in boiling water, containing about five pounds of common brown sugar per gallon. Then pack, when cool, small ends down, in an intimate mixture of one part of finely powdered charcoal and two of dry bran. In this way they will last six months or more. The scalding water causes the formation of a thin skin of hard albumen near the inner surface of the shell, and the sugar of syrup closes all the pores."

The Scientific American neglects, however, to add that when you open them six months after they were picked and preserved, the safest way is to open them out in the alley with a revolver, at sixteen paces. When you have succeeded in opening one, you can jump on a fleet horse and get out of the country before the nut brown flavor catches up with you.

(*Baled Hay*, 1884)

Regarding the Nose

The annals of surgery contain many cases where the nose has been cut or torn off, and being replaced has grown fast again, recovering its jeopardized functions. One of the earliest, 1680, is related by the surgeon (Fioraventi) who happened to be nearby when a man's nose, having been cut off, had fallen in the sand. He remarks that he took it up, washed it, replaced it, and that it grew together.

Still, this is a little bit hazardous, and in warm weather the nose might refuse to catch on. It would be mortifying in the extreme to have the nose drop off in a dish of ice-cream at a large banquet. Not only would it be disagreeable to the owner of the nose, but to those who sat near him.

He adds the address of the owner of the repaired nose, and requests any doubter to go and examine for himself. Regnault, in the *Gazette Salutaire*, 1714, tells of a patient whose nose was bitten off by a smuggler. The owner of the nose wrapped it in a bit of cloth and sought Regnault, who, "although the part was cold, reset it, and it became attached."

This is another instance where, by being sufficiently previous, the nose was secured and handed down to future generations. Yet, as we said before, it is a little bit risky, and a nose of that character cannot be relied upon at all times. After a nose has once seceded it cannot be expected to still adhere to the old constitution with such loyalty as prior to that change.

Although these cases call for more credulity than most of us have to spare, yet later cases, published in trustworthy journals, would seem to corroborate this. In the *Clinical Annals* and *Medical Gazette*, of Heidelberg, 1830, there are sixteen similar cases cited by the surgeon (Dr. Hofacker) who was appointed by the senate to attend the duels of the students.

It seems that during these duels it is not uncommon for a student to slice off the nose of his adversary, and lay it on the table until the duel is over. After that the surgeon puts it on with mucilage and it never misses a meal, but keeps right on growing.

The wax nose is attractive, but in a warm room it is apt to get excited and wander down into the mustache, or it may stray away under the collar, and when the proprietor goes to wipe this feature he does not wipe anything but space. A gold nose that opens on one side and is engraved, with hunter case and key wind, is attractive, especially on a bright day. The coin-silver nose is very well in its way, but rather commonplace unless designed to match the tea service and the knives and forks. In that case, good taste is repaid by admiration and pleasure on the part of the guest.

The *papier-maché* nose is durable and less liable to become cold and disagreeable. It is also lighter and not liable to season crack.

False noses are made of *papier-maché*, leather, gold, silver and wax. These last are fitted to spectacles or springs, and are difficult to distinguish from a true nose.

Tycho Brahe lost his nose in a duel and wore a golden one, which he attached to his face with cement, which he always carried about.

This was a good scheme, as it found him always prepared for accidents. He could, at any moment, repair to a dressing room, or even slide into an alley where he could avoid the prying gaze of the vulgar world, and glue his nose on. Of course he ran the risk of getting it on crooked and a little out of line with his other features, but this would naturally only attract attention and fix the minds of those with whom he might be called upon to converse. A man with his nose glued on wrong side up, could hold the attention of an audience for hours, when any other man would seem tedious and uninteresting.

(*Baled Hay*, 1884)

Is Dueling Murder?

Somebody wants to know whether dueling is murder, and we reply in clarion tones that it depends largely on how fatal it is. Dueling with monogram note paper, at a distance of 1,200 yards, is not murder.

(*Baled Hay*, 1884)

About the Autopsy

We have been carefully reading and investigating the report of Dr. Lamb, relative to the anatomical condition of the late remnants of Charles J. Guiteau, and also a partial or minority report furnished by the other two doctors, who got on their ear at the time of the autopsy. We are permitted to print the fragment of a private letter addressed personally to the editor from one of these gentlemen, whose name we are not permitted to use. He says:

"We found the late lamented, and after looking him over thoroughly, and removing what works he had inside of him, agreed, almost at once, that he was dead. This was the only point upon which we agreed.

"Shortly after we began to remove the internal economy of the deceased, some little discussion arose between Doc Lamb and myself about the extravasation of blood in the right pectoralis and the peculiar position of the dewflicker on the dome of the diaphragm. I made a suggestion about the causes that had led to this, stating, in my opinion, the pericarditis had crossed the median line and congested the dewdad.

"He said it was no such thing, and that I didn't know the difference between a malpighian capsule and an abdominal viscera.

"That insulted me, but I held my temper, going on with my work, removing the gall-bladder and other things, as though nothing had been said.

"By and by, Lamb said I'd better quit fooling with the pancreas, and come and help him. Then he advanced a tomfool theory about an adhesion of the dura mater to the jibboom, or some medical rot or other, and I told him that I thought he was wrong, and I didn't believe deceased had any dura mater. Lamb flared up then, and struck at me with a bloody towel. I then grabbed a fragment of liver, and pasted him in the nose. I don't allow any sawbone upstart to impose on me, if I know it. He then called me a very opprobrious epithet, indeed, and struck me in the eye with a kidney. Then the fight became disgraceful, and by the time we got through, the late lamented was considerably scattered. Here lay a second-hand lobe of liver, while over there was the apex of a lung hanging on a gas fixture. It was a pretty lively scrimmage, and made quite a feeling between us. I still think, however, that I was right in standing up for my theory and when an old pelican like Lamb thinks he can scare me into St. Vitus' dance, he fools himself. The fact is, he don't know a gall-bladder from the gout, and he couldn't tell a lobulated tumor from the side of a house. I told him so, too, while I was putting some court plaster on my nose, after he pasted me with an old prison bedstead. Lamb would get along better with me if he would curb his violent temper. I guess he thought so, too, when I broke his false teeth and jammed them so far back into his oesophagus that he got blue in the face. I never allow a second-hand horse doctor to impose on me, if I know it, and it is time Doc Lamb took a grand aborescent tumble to himself."

(*Baled Hay*, 1884)

Etiquette of the Napkin

It has been stated, and very truly too, that the law of the napkin is but vaguely understood. It may be said, however, on the start, that custom and good breeding have uttered the decree that it is in poor taste to put the napkin in the pocket and carry it away.

The rule of etiquette is becoming more and more thoroughly established, that the napkin should be left at the house of the host or hostess, after dinner.

There has been a good deal of discussion, also, upon the matter of folding the napkin after dinner, and whether it should be so disposed of, or negligently tossed into the gravy boat. If, however, it can be folded easily, and without attracting too much attention and prolonging the session for several hours, it should be so arranged, and placed beside the plate, where it may be easily found by the hostess, and returned to her neighbor from whom she borrowed it for the occasion. If, however, the lady of the house is not doing her own work, the napking may be carefully jammed into a globular wad, and fired under the table, to convey the idea of utter recklessness and pampered abandon.

The use of the finger bowl is also a subject of much importance to the bon ton guest who gorges himself at the expense of his friends.

The custom of drinking out of the finger bowl, though not entirely obsolete, has been limited to the extent that good breeding does not now permit the guest to quaff the water from his finger bowl, unless he does so prior to using it as a finger bowl.

Thus it will be seen that social customs are slowly but surely cutting down and circumscribing the rights and privileges of the masses.

At the court of Eugenie, the customs of the table were very rigid, and the most prominent guest of H. R. H. was liable to get the G. B. if he spread his napkin on his nap, and cut his egg in two with a carving knife. The custom was that the napkin should be hung on one knee, and the egg busted at the big end and scooped out with a spoon.

A prominent American, at her table, one day, in an unguarded moment, shattered the shell of a soft-boiled egg with his knife, and, while prying it apart, both thumbs were erroneously jammed into the true inwardness of the fruit with so much momentum that the juice took him in the eye, thus blinding him and maddening him to such a degree, that he got up and threw the remnants into the bosom of the hired man plenipotentiary, who stood near the table, scratching his ear with a tray. As may readily be supposed, there was a painful interim during which it was hard to tell for five or six minutes whether the prominent American or the hired man would come out on top; but at last the American, with the egg in his eye, got the ear of the high-priced hired man in among his back teeth, and the honor of our beloved flag was vindicated.

(*Baled Hay*, 1884)

A Thrilling Experience

I had a very thrilling experience the other evening. I had just filled an engagement in a strange city, and retired to my cozy room at the hotel.

The thunders of applause had died away, and the opera house had been locked up to await the arrival of an Uncle Tom's Cabin Company. The last loiterer had returned to his home, and the lights in the palace of the pork packer were extinguished.

No sound was heard, save the low, tremulous swash of the sleet outside or the death-rattle in the throat of the bath tub. Then all was still as the bosom of a fried chicken when the spirit has departed.

The swallow-tail coat hung limp and weary in the wardrobe, and the gross receipts of the evening were under my pillow. I needed sleep, for I was worn out with travel and anxiety, but the fear of being robbed kept me from repose. I know how desperate a man becomes when he yearns for another's gold. I know how cupidity drives a wicked man to mangle his victim that he may win precarious prosperity and how he will often take a short cut to wealth by means of murder, when, if he would enter politics, he might accomplish his purpose as surely and much more safely.

Anon, however, tired nature succumbed. I know I had succumbed, for the bell-boy afterward testified that he heard me do so.

The gentle warmth of the steam-heated room and the comforting assurance of duty well done and the approval of friends at last lulled me into a gentle repose.

Anyone who might have looked upon me, as I lay there in that innocent slumber, with the winsome mouth slightly ajar and the playful limbs cast wildly about, while a merry smile now and then flitted across the regular features, would have said that no heart could be so hard as to harbor ill for one so guileless and so simple.

I do not know what it was that caused me to wake. Some slight sound or other, no doubt, broke my slumber, and I opened my eyes wildly. The room was in semi-darkness.

Hark!

A slight movement in the corner, and the low, regular breathing of a human being! I was now wide awake. Possibly I could have opened my eyes wider, but not without spilling them out of their sockets.

Regularly came that soft, low breathing. Each time it seemed like a sigh of relief, but it did not relieve me. Evidently it was not done for that purpose. It sounded like a sigh of blessed relief, such as a woman might heave after she has returned from church and transferred herself from the embrace of her new Russia iron, black silk dress into a friendly wrapper.

Regularly, like the rise and fall of a wave on the summer sea, it rose and fell, while my pale lambrequin of hair rose and fell fitfully with it.

I know that people who read this will laugh at it, but there was nothing to laugh at. At first I feared that the sigh might be that of a woman who had entered the room through a transom in order to see me, as I lay wrapt in slumber, and then carry the picture away to gladden her whole life.

But no. That was hardly possible. It was cupidity that had driven some cruel villain to enter my apartments and to crouch in the gloom till the proper moment should come in which to spring upon me, throttle me, crowd a hotel pillow into each lung, and while I did the Desdemona act, rob me of my hard-earned wealth.

Regularly still rose the soft breathing as though the robber might be trying to suppress it. I reached gently under the pillow, and securing the money I put it in the pocket of my *robe de nuit*. Then, with great care, I pulled out a copy of Smith & Wesson's great work on "How to Ventilate the Human Form." I said to myself that I would sell my life as dearly as possible, so that whoever bought it would always regret the trade.

Then I opened the volume at the first chapter and addressed a thirty-eight calibre remark in the direction of the breath in the corner.

When the echoes had died away a sigh of relief welled up from the dark corner. Also another sigh of relief later on.

I then decided to light the gas and fight it out. You have no doubt seen a man scratch a match on the leg of his pantaloons. Perhaps you have also seen an absent-minded man undertake to do so, forgetting that his pantaloons were hanging on a chair at the other end of the room.

However, I lit the gas with my left hand and kept my revolver pointed toward the dark corner where the breath was still rising and falling.

People who had heard my lecture came rushing in, hoping to find that I had suicided, but they found that, instead of humoring the public in that way, I had shot the valve off the steam radiator.

It is humiliating to write the foregoing myself, but I would rather do so than have the affair garbled by careless hands.

(*Bill Nye's Remarks*, 1887)

Answers to Correspondents

Caller.—Your calling cards should be modest as to size and neatly engraved, with an extra flourish.

In calling, there are two important things to be considered: First, when to call, and, second, when to rise and hang on the door handle.

Some make one-third of the call before rising, and then complete the call while airing the house and holding the door open, while others consider this low and vulgar, making at least one-fourth of the call in the hall, and one-half between the front door and the gate. Different authorities differ as to the proper time for calling. Some think you should not call before 3 or after 5 P.M., but if you have had any experience and had ordinary sense to start with, you will know when to call as soon as you look at your hand.

Amateur Prize Fighter.—The boxing glove is a large upholstered buckskin mitten, with an abnormal thumb and a string by which it is attached to the wrist, so that when you feed it to an adversary he cannot swallow it and choke himself. There are two kinds of gloves, viz., hard gloves and soft gloves.

I once fought with soft gloves to a finish with a young man who was far my inferior intellectually, but he exceeded me in brute force and knowledge of the use of the gloves. He was not so tall, but he was wider than myself. Longitudinally he was my inferior, but latitudinally he outstripped me. We did not fight a regular prize-fight. It was just done for pleasure. But I do not think we should abandon ourselves entirely to pleasure. It is enervating and makes one eye swell up and turn blue.

I still think that a young man ought to have a knowledge of the manly art of self-defense, and if I could acquire such a knowledge without getting into a fight about it I would surely learn how to defend myself.

The boxing glove is worn on the hand of one party, and on the gory nose of the other party as the game progresses. Soft gloves very rarely kill anyone, unless they work down into the bronchial tubes and shut off the respiration.

Lecturer, New York City.—You need not worry so much about your costume until you have written your lecture, and it would be a good idea to test the public a little, if possible, before you do much expensive printing. Your idea seems to be that a man should get a fine lithograph of himself and a $100 suit of clothes, and then write his lecture to fit the lithograph and the clothes. That is erroneous.

You say that you have written a part of your lecture,

but do not feel satisfied with it. In this you will no doubt find many people who will agree with you.

You could wear a full dress suit of black with propriety, or a Prince Albert coat with your hand thrust into the bosom of it. I once lectured on the subject of phrenology in the southern portion of Utah, being at that time temporarily busted, but still hoping to tide over the dull times by delivering a lecture on the subject of "Brains, and how to detect their presence." I was not supplied with a phrenological bust at that time, and as such a thing is almost indispensable, I borrowed a young man from Provost and induced him to act as bust for the evening. He did so with thrilling effect, taking the entire gross receipts of the lecture course from my pocket while I was illustrating the effect of alcoholic stimulants on the raw brain of an adult in a state of health.

You can remove spots of egg from your full dress suit with ammonia and water, applied by means of a common nail brush. You do not ask for this recipe, but, judging from your style, I hope that it may be of use to you.

Martin F. Tupper, Texas.—The poem to which you allude was written by Julia A. Moore, better known as the Sweet Singer of Michigan. The last stanza was something like this:

> "My childhood days are past and gone,
>   And it fills my heart with pain,
> To think that youth will nevermore
>   Return to me again.
> And now, kind friends, what I have wrote,
>   I hope you will pass o'er
> And not criticise as some has done, hitherto
>   herebefore."

Miss Moore also wrote a volume of poems which the farmers of Michigan are still using on their potato bugs. She wrote a large number of poems, all more or less saturated with grief and damaged syntax. She is now said to be a fugitive from justice. We should learn from this that we cannot evade the responsibility of our acts, and those who write obituary poetry will one day be overtaken by a bob-tail sleuth hound or a Siberian nemesis with two rows of teeth.

Alonzo G., Smithville.—Yes, you can learn three card monte without a master. It is very easy. The book will cost you twenty-five cents and then you can practice on various people. The book is a very small item, you will find, after you have been practicing awhile. Three card monte and justifiable homicide go hand in hand. 2. You can turn a jack from the bottom of the pack in the old sledge, if you live in some States, but west of the Missouri the air is so light that men who have tried it have frequently waked up on the shore of eternity with a half turned jack in their hand and a hole in the cerebellum the size of an English walnut.

You can get "Poker and Three Card Monte without a Master" for sixty cents, with a coroner's verdict thrown in. If you contemplate a career as a monte man, you should wear a pair of low, loose shoes that you can kick off easily, unless you want to die with your boots on.

Henry Ubet, Montana.—No, you are mistaken in your assumption that Socrates was the author of the maxim to which you allude. It is of more modern origin and, in fact, the sentence of which you speak, viz: "What a combination of conflicting and paradoxical assertions is life? Of what use are logic and argument when we find the true inwardness of the bologna sausage on the outside?" were written by a philosopher who is still living. I am willing to give Socrates credit for what he has said and done, but when I think of a sentiment that is worthy to be graven on a monolith and passed on down to prosperity, I do not want to have it attributed to such men as Socrates.

Leonora Vivian Gobb, Oleson's Forks, Ariz.—Yes. You can turn the front breadths, let out the tucks in the side plaiting and baste on a new dagoon where you caught the oyster stew in your lap at the party. You could also get trusted for a new dress, perhaps. But that is a matter of taste. Some dealers are wearing their open accounts long this winter and some are not. Do as you think best about cleaning the dress. Benzine will sometimes eradicate an oyster stew from dress goods. It will also eradicate everyone in the room at the same time. I have known a pair of rejuvenated kid gloves to break up a funeral that started out with every prospect of success. Benzine is an economical thing to use, but socially it is not up to the standard. Another idea has occurred to me, however. Why not riprap the skirt, calk the selvages, readjust the box plaits, cat stitch the crown sheet, file down the gores, sandpaper the gaiters and discharge the dolman. You could then wear the garment anywhere in the evening, and half the people wouldn't know anything had happened to it.

James, Owatonna, Minn.—You can easily teach yourself to play on the tuba. You know what Shakespeare says: "Tuba or not tuba? That's the question."

How true this is? It touches every heart. It is as good a soliloquy as I ever read. P. S. Please do not swallow the tuba while practicing and choke yourself to death. It would be a shame for you to swallow a nice new tuba and cast a gloom over it so that no one else would ever want to play on it again.

Florence.—You can stimulate your hair by using castor oil three ounces, brandy one ounce. Put the oil on the sewing machine, and absorb the brandy between meals. The brandy will no doubt fly right to your head and either greatly assist your hair or it will reconcile you to your lot. The great attraction about brandy as a hair tonic is that it should not build up the thing. If you wish, you may drink the brandy and then breathe hard on the scalp. This will be difficult at first but after a while it will not seem irksome.

(*Bill Nye's Remarks*, 1887)

Prying Open the Future

"Ring the bell and the door will open," is the remark made by a small label over a bell-handle in Third avenue, near Eighteenth street, where Mme. La Foy reads the past, present and future at so much per read. Love, marriage, divorce, illness, speculation and sickness are there handled with the utmost impunity by "Mme. La Foy, the famous scientific astrologist," who has monkeyed with the planets for twenty years, and if she wanted any information has "read it in the stars."

I rang the bell the other day to see if the door would open. It did so after considerable delay, and a pimply boy in knee pants showed me upstairs into the waiting-room. After a while I was removed to the consultation-room, where Mme. La Foy, seated behind a small oil-cloth covered table, rakes up old personalities and pries into the future at cut rates.

Skirmishing about among the planets for twenty years involves a great deal of fatigue and exposure, to say nothing of the night work, and so Mme. La Foy has the air of one who has put in a very busy life. She is as familiar with planets though as you or I might be with our own family, and calls them by their first names. She would know Jupiter, Venus, Saturn, Adonis or any of the other fixed stars the darkest night that ever blew.

"Mme. La Foy De Graw," said I, bowing with the easy grace of a gentleman of the old school, "would you mind peering into the future for me about a half dollars' worth, not necessarily for publication, et cetera."

"Certainly not. What would you like to know?"

"Why, I want to know all I can for the money," I said in a bantering tone. "Of course I do not wish to know what I already know. It is what I do not now know that I desire to know. Tell me what I do not know, Madame. I will detain you but a moment."

She gave me back my large, round half dollar and told me that she was already weary. She asked me to excuse her. She was willing to unveil the future to me in her poor, weak way, but she could not guarantee to let a large flood of light into the darkened basement of a benighted mind for half a dollar.

"You can tell me what year and on what day of what month you were born," said Mme. La Foy, "and I will outline your life to you. I generally require a lock of the hair, but in your case we will dispense with it."

I told her when I was born and the circumstances as well as I could recall them.

"This brings you under Venus, Mercury and Mars. These three planets were in conjunction at the time of your birth. You were born when the sign was wrong and you have had more or less trouble ever since. Had you been born when the sign was in the head or the heart, instead of the feet, you would not have spread out over the ground so much.

"Your health is very good, as is the health of those generally who are born under the same auspices that you were. People who are born under the reign of the crab are apt to be cancerous. You, however, have great lung power and wonderful gastric possibilities. Yet, at times, you would be easily upset. A strong cyclone that would unroof a court-house or tip over a through train would also upset you, in spite of your broad, firm feet if the wind got behind one of your ears.

"You will be married early and you will be very happy, though your wife will not enjoy herself very much. Your wife will be much happier during her second marriage.

"You will prosper better in business matters without forming any partnerships. Do not go into partnership with a small, dark man who has neuralgia and a fine yacht. He has abundant means, but he will go through you like an electric shock.

"Tuesdays and Saturdays will be your most fortunate

days on which to borrow money of men with light hair. Mondays and Thursdays will be your best days for approaching dark men.

"Look out for a low-sot man accompanied by an office cat, both of whom are engaged in the newspaper business. He is crafty and bald-headed on his father's side. He prints the only paper that contains the full text of his speeches at testimonials and dinners given to other people. Do not loan him money on any account.

"You will succeed well as a musician or an inventor, but you would not do well as a poet. You have all the keen sensibility and strong passion of a poet, but you haven't the hair. Do not try poesy.

"In the future I see you very prosperous. You are on the lecture platform speaking. Large crowds of people are jostling each other at the box-office and trying to get their money back.

"Then I see you riding behind a flexible horse that must have cost a large sum of money. You are smoking a cigar that has never been in use before. Then Venus bisects the orbit of Mars and I see you going home with your head tied up in the lap robe, you and your spirited horse in the same ambulance."

"But do you see anything for me in the future, Mme. La Foy?" I asked, taking my feet off the table, the better to watch her features; "anything that would seem to indicate political preferment, a reward for past services to my country, as it were?"

"No, not clearly. But wait a moment. Your horoscope begins to get a little more intelligent. I see you at the door of the Senate Chamber. You are counting over your money and looking sadly at a schedule of prices. Then you turn sorrowfully away and decide to buy a seat in the House instead. Many years after I see you in the Senate. You are there day after day attending to your duties. You are there early, before any one else, and I see you pacing back and foth, up and down the aisles, sweeping out the Senate

Chamber and dusting off the seats and rejuvenating the cuspidors."

"Does this horoscope which you are using this season give you any idea as to whether money matters will be scarce with me next week or otherwise, and if so what I had better do about it?"

"Towards the last of the week you will experience considerable monetary prostration, but just as you have become despondent, at the very tail end of the week, the horizon will clear up and a slight, dark gentleman, with wide trousers, who is a total stranger to you, will loan you quite a sum of money, with the understanding that it is to be repaid on Monday."

"Then you would not advise me to go to Coney Island until the week after next?"

"Certainly not."

"Would it be etiquette in dancing a quadrille to swing a young person of the opposite sex twice round at a select party when you are but slightly acquainted, but feel quite confident that her partner is unarmed?"

"Yes."

"Does your horoscope tell a person what to do with raspberry jelly that will not jell?"

"No, not at the present prices."

"So you predict an early marriage, with threatening weather and strong prevailing easterly winds along the Gulf States?"

"Yes, sir."

"And is there no way that this early marriage may be evaded?"

"No, not unless you put it off till later in life."

"Thank you," I said, rising and looking out the window over a broad sweep of undulating alley and wind-swept roofing, "and now, how much are you out on this?"

"Sir!"

"What's the damage?"

"Oh, one dollar."

"But don't you advertise to read the past, present and future for fifty cents?"

"Well, that is where a person has had other information before in his life and has some knowledge to begin with; but where I fill up a vacant mind entirely and store it with facts of all kinds and stock it up so that it can do business for itself, I charge a dollar. I cannot thoroughly refit and refurnish a mental tenement from the ground up for fifty cents."

I do not think we have as good "Astrologists" now as we used to have. Astrologists cannot crawl under the tent and pry into the future as they could three or four thousand years ago.

(*Nye and Riley's Railway Guide*, 1888)

Hints for the Household

There are a great many pleasures to which we may treat ourselves very economically if we go at it right. In this way we can, at a slight expense, have those comforts, and even luxuries, for which we should otherwise pay a great price.

Costly rugs and carpets, though beautiful and rich in appearance, involve such an outlay of money that many hesitate about buying them; but a very tasty method of treating floors inexpensively consists in staining the edge for several feet in width, leaving the center of the room to be covered by a large rug. Staining for the floor may be easily made, by boiling maple bark, twenty parts; poke-berry juice, twenty-five parts; hazel brush, thirty parts, and sour milk, twenty-five parts, until it becomes about the consistency of the theory of infant damnation. Let it stand a few weeks, until the rich flavor has died down, so that you can look at it for quite a while without nausea; then add vinegar and copperas to suit the taste, and apply by means of a whisk broom. When dry, help yourself to some more of it. This gives the floor a rich pauper's coffin shade, over which shellac or cod liver oil should be applied.

Rugs may be made of coffee sacking or Turkish gunny-rest sacks, inlaid with rich designs in red yarn, and a handsome fringe can be added by raveling the edges.

A beautiful receptable for soiled collars and cuffs may be made by putting a cardboard bottom in a discarded and shattered coal scuttle, gilding the whole and tying a pale blue ribbon on the bail.

A cheap and very handsome easy-chair can be constructed by sawing into a flour barrel and removing less than half the length of staves for one-third the distance around, then fasten inside a canvas or duck seat, below which the barrel is filled with bran.

A neat little mackerel tub makes a most appropriate foot-stool for this chair, and looks so unconventional and rustic that it wins every one at once. Such a chair should also have a limited number of tidies on its surface. Otherwise it might give too much satisfaction. A good style of inexpensive tidy is made by poking holes in some heavy, strong goods, and then darning up these holes with something else. The darned tidy holds its place better, I think, and is more frequently worn away on the back of the last guest than any other.

This list might be prolonged almost indefinitely, and I should be glad to write my own experience in the line of experiment, if it were not for the danger of appearing egotistical. For instance, I once economized in the matter of paper-hanging, deciding that I would save the paper-hanger's bill and put the money into preferred trotting stock.

So I read a recipe in a household hint, which went on to state how one should make and apply paste to wall paper, how to begin, how to apply the paper, and all that. The paste was made by uniting flour, water and glue in such a way as to secure the paper to the wall and yet leave it smooth, according to the recipe. First the walls had to be "sized," however.

I took a tape-measure and sized the walls.

Next I began to prepare the paste and cook some in a large milk-pan. It looked very repulsive indeed, but it looked so much better than it smelled, that I did not mind. Then I put about five cents' worth of it on one roll of paper, and got up on a chair to begin. My idea was to apply it to the wall mostly, but the chair tipped, and so I papered the piano and my wife on the way down. My wife gasped for breath, but soon tore a hole through the paper so she could breathe, and then she laughed at me. That is the reason I took another end of the paper and repapered her face. I can not bear to have any one laugh at me when I am myself unhappy.

It was good paste, if you merely desired to disfigure a piano or a wife, but otherwise it would not stick at all. I did not like it. I was mad about it. But my wife seemed quite stuck on it. She hasn't got it all out of her hair yet.

Then a man dropped in to see me about some money that I had hoped to pay him that morning, and he said the paste needed more glue and a quart of molasses. I put in some more glue and the last drop of molasses we had in the house. I made a mass which looked like unbaked ginger snaps, and smelled as I imagined the deluge did at low tide.

I next proceeded to paper the room. Sometimes the paper would adhere, and then again it would refrain from adhering. When I got around the room I had gained ground so fast at the top and lost so much time at the bottom of the walls, that I had to put in a wedge of paper two feet wide at the bottom, and tapering to a point at the top, in order to cover the space. This gave the room the appearance of having been toyed with by an impatient cyclone, or an air of inebriety not in keeping with my poor but honest character.

I went to bed very weary, and abraded in places. I had paste in my pockets, and bronze up my nose. In the night I could hear the paper crack. Just as I would get almost to sleep, it would pop. That was because the paper was contracting and trying to bring the dimensions of the room I own to fit it.

In the morning the room had shrunken so that the carpet did not fit, and the paper hung in large molasses-covered welts on the walls. It looked real grotesque. I got a paper-hanger to come and look at it. He did so.

"And what would you advise me to do with it, sir?" I asked, with a degree of deference which I had never before shown to a paper-hanger.

"Well, I can hardly say at first. It is a very bad case. You see, the glue and stuff have made the paper and wrinkles so hard now, that it would cost a great deal to blast it off. Do you own the house?"

"Yes, sir. That is, I have paid one-half the purchase-price, and there is a mortgage for the balance."

"Oh. Well, then you are all right," said the paper-hanger, with a gleam of hope in his eye. "Let it go on the mortgage."

Then I had to economize again, so I next resorted to the home method of administering the Turkish bath. You can get a Turkish bath in that way at a cost of four and one-half to five cents, which is fully as good as one that will cost you a dollar or more in some places.

I read the directions in a paper. There are two methods of administering the low-price Turkish bath at home. One consists in placing the person to be treated in a cane-seat chair, and then putting a pan of hot water beneath this chair. Ever and anon a hot stone or hot flat-iron is dropped into the water by means of tongs, and thus the water is kept boiling, the steam rising in thick masses about the person in the chair, who is carefully concealed in a large blanket. Every time a hot flat-iron or stone is dropped into the pan it spatters the boiling water on the bare limbs of the person who is being operated upon, and if you are living in the same country with him, you will hear him loudly wrecking his chances beyond the grave by stating things that are really wrong.

The other method, and the one I adopted, is better than this. You apply the heat by menas of a spirit lamp, and no one, to look at a little fifteen cent spirit lamp, would believe that it had so much heat in it till he has had one under him as he sits in a wicker chair.

A wicker chair does not interfere with the lamp at all, or cut off the heat, and one is so swathed in blankets and rubber overcoats that he can't help himself.

I seated myself in that way, and then the torch was applied. Did the reader ever get out of a bath and sit down on a wire brush in order to put on his shoes, and feel a sort of startled thrill pervade his whole being? Well, that is good enough as far as it goes, but it does not really count as a sensation, when you have been through the Home Treatment Turkish Bath.

My wife was in another room reading a new book in which she was greatly interested. While she was thus storing her mind with information, she thought she smelled something burning. She went all around over the house trying to find out what it was. Finally she found out.

It was her husband. I called to her, of course, but she wanted me to wait until she had discovered what was on fire. I tried to tell her to come and search my neighborhood, but I presume I did not make myself understood, because I was excited, and my personal epidermis was being singed off in a way that may seem to funny to others, but was not so to one who had to pass through it.

It bored me quite a deal. Once the wicker seat of the chair caught fire.

"Oh, heavens," I cried, with a sudden pang of horror, "am I to be thus devoured by the fire fiend? And is there no one to help? Help! Help! Help!"

I also made use of other expressions but they did not add to the sense of the above.

I perspired very much, indeed, and so the bath was, in a

measure, a success, but oh, what doth it profit a man to gain a bath if he lose his own soul?

(*A Guest at the Ludlow*, 1897)

Bill Nye Consults a Phrenologist and Is Exposed

In order to note the advancement made by the great science of phrenology in the past thirty years, I went yesterday to visit the leading phrenologist of the United States, and no doubt of the world. Frankly, I must confess that it was a case of going quietly to scoff and remaining to pray, for I don't believe that Inspector Byrnes is "on to me" with more fidelity or accuracy than the venerable bump manipulator of Broadway, who has been at it for forty-five years, and who turned me over yesterday.

There is one thing about me which arouses my admiration, and that is that when I am detected and overtaken and discovered in the delictu business and handcuffed to a large cook stove I know enough to surrender. I am not hidebound, but always open to conviction and sentence.

Thirty years ago I took my mother to a phrenologist to have her head looked over, feeling that as a parent she was not proving the success that I had hoped for, and after I had counted out six dozen eggs for him, which I had brought to pay him for the work, he offered to examine my head and give me a written schedule of it for two pounds of butter which I still had left over.

He wanted to please my mother, and so he spoke highly of my talents—higher than they deserved, I think. He was a plain man, with a stern and rocky air, like that of one who has been playing the first act of "The Prodigal Son" all his life, and waiting for the letter that never came, asking him home to spend the holidays.

He said I had a high "forward," which reminded him of that of Daniel Webster, whom he once examined. I said that we were often mistaken for one another.

This phrenologist had a very hairy and Castle Garden air, and when his paper collar peeped out from his jungle of common, plastering hair you could see that when he liked a collar he stuck to it.

Phrenology where I lived in those days had hardly risen to the position of a science. It was merely a "job." This man, whom I will call Professor Biltong, had to combine other things with his phrenology, such as chiropody and the sale of fruit trees. Phrenology at that time was found often combined with astrology and phlebotomy.

In those days men had not learned to add physiognomy and a general knowledge of human nature to the science of phrenology, and thus read a man as we would read a hotel register.

It was for that reason, perhaps, that Professor Biltong erred in reading me with a far away look, and marking out for me a future occupation to which I was best adapted.

Possibly it may interest the reader, especially the boy or young man who reads this, if I tell him briefly how Professor Biltong erred in my case, and how he caused me thereby much annoyance and would have cost me a great deal of money if I had had it at the time. If any one can be led to profit by my errors and thus dodge them at my expense I am only too glad to aid him.

Professor Biltong said that I would make a powerful and eloquent lawyer. He said that alimentiveness, ideality and secretiveness were just the right size to make a good lawyer, and that with the Websterian dashboard which I had, coupled with great inhabitiveness, could not fail to jar the entire structure of the bar, together with the crackers and cheese standing on the end thereof.

He rambled around over the site where my hair was waving a long farewell to friends and kindred, and he said, as I looked up boylike into his massive and somewhat self-made whiskers: "You would make a good United States Senator if you had the means, but you would make a better lawyer. It is better to be a good lawyer than a poor Senator. Besides, it will take a good many eggs at the present price to get you to the Senate, and long before you received your credentials your poor overworked hens would curl up in their inlaid nests and quit.

"So let us not think of going to the Senate. Possibly we can find some one else to go. You had better be a lawyer. Your caution and love of approbation would keep you out of the penitentiary, and at the same time win the approval of your clients and the jury. Your voice is magnetic, and your physique of that peculiar flexible, mobile and reversible order which would look well stuffed.

"Do not despair, but go in to win. You would make a very good piano tuner, of course, having a wealth of ear, but lacking in quality; but you have the proper integument of skull, the sinuosites of cerebral convolutions, the philoprogenitiveness, the awe, the self-esteem and the combativeness necessary to make you a good lawyer, and one who will make himself felt and known from the tough and rocky shores of your New England birthplace to the dimpled feet of the snow-capped Sierras."

With that he ceased, and saying that it was his hour for dinner, he took from his pocket a copy of the Boston Whig, inclosing a cheese sandwich and large, warty cucumber pickle cut in half, and began to stow it away among his beard.

I at once proceeded to prepare myself for the law. First I had to brush up a little in long division and spelling. This I did by taking a preparatory course at the Tidd school. This was called the Tidd school because it was endowed by him during the plum season, without his knowledge, however, and we carried water from his well to quench the never dying thirst of the school.

Closing my term there with high honors and a baritone voice, which I cannot account for to this day, I got a place to study law and tidy up the cuspidors for a country lawyer whose name and memory are green and beautiful yet in the warmest corner of my heart.

While I did not make a lawyer of myself, it was not his fault. It was my own. And Biltong should have told me on the start. That's what I paid him for. But in those days every boy who wore a big hat and got tired easily with manual toil was set aside for the ministry or the law. That's why so many sleeping cars are attached to the gospel trains today, and so many lawyers hang by the gills to politics and eat rump steak with thankful hearts.

Listening to the siren song of Professor Biltong, I read Blackstone all one summer and his thrilling remarks about the right of piscary and the fee simple and fee tail and seisin which marred the history of the common law of England. I tried, oh, so hard, to cuddle up to Justinian and to get intimate with Coke, and to enjoy commons of Estorers and commons of Turbary.

Meantime I swept out the office, ran the errands, got my board bill and trousers receipted, and looked forward to the time when I should shake the resolution of the most stubborn and strong-hearted juror that ever drew his little old $2 a day.

Days grew into weeks, weeks expanded into years. I was still reading one day what I easily forgot the next, thus storing my youthful mind with large quantities of echoing space which have since been very useful to me for other purposes.

Now came the time, after two years of this sort of work, when people thought I ought to be "admitted." They talked as if it would be purely a matter of form; that I ought not to wait, for every moment I stayed outside of the profession was a loss to the American people.

The committee did not seem to think so. I went away by stage to a desolate and threadbare county seat somewhere, and laid out my little stock of unripe knowledge before that committee, and they sampled it one after another and gently took me one side, and instead of telling me, as they might, most truthfully, to go home and never fool with the law any more, they hated to hurt my feelings, and so they told me to study some more on this point and brush up on that, and so on.

So I returned, sold a pet heifer, and buying a set of Kent's Commentaries and a nice warm pair of kip boots, read another six months and did general janitor work around the office, also drawing deeds, mortgages and portraits of the senior member of the firm.

At the end of that time I began to think I ought to get examined again. Every spring and fall term I would go through this ordeal, and then get bound over for examination the following term. Finally it got to be a part of the calendar. When the court was waiting for a witness or a juror it would put in the time by examining me.

This ran on for some time, till I got tired of it and fled. In a new field, where the officials were being appointed by the President, and some of them knew less even than I did, I felt at home right away, and finally one glad day in summer, with a joyful heart, though with many scars on the places where previous committees had knocked the bark off my soul, I signed the book and became a lawyer.

One of the old committee has kindly told me since that it made his heart bleed to refuse me, and that if he'd known how little damage I would do as a lawyer, and how quiet I'd have been about it, blamed if he wouldn't have suspended the rules in my case and moved my admission.

Now I do not blame phrenology for this, but Professor Biltong, who should have seen that while I had some of the prerequisites for a lawyer, I lacked one great essential, and that was the ability to repeat a law, a ruling or a definition in the exact language of anybody else.

That ignorance on his part cost me many a reluctant, evasive and finally tear-dimmed dollar, and came very near landing me in the lap of an overworked and overburdened public, one of the most pitiful objects known to the entomologists, viz., a pettifogger.

If this letter were not already too personal I would add the stenographic and geological report made on my head yesterday. It is so accurate that it reminds me almost of the old days of necromancy, whatever that is.

(*The Funny Fellows Grab-Bag*, 1903)